Family, Women, and Socialization
in the Kibbutz

Family, Women, and Socialization in the Kibbutz

Menachem Gerson
The Institute of Research on
Kibbutz Education, Oranim

Lexington Books
D.C. Heath and Company
Lexington, Massachusetts
Toronto

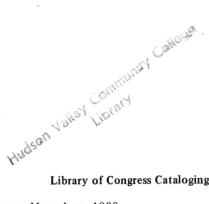

Library of Congress Cataloging in Publication Data

Gerson, Menachem, 1908–
    Family, women, and socialization in the kibbutz.

    Includes index.
    1. Collective settlements—Israel. 2. Family—Israel. 3. Women—Israel.
I. Title.
HX742.2.A3G47   334′.683′095694   78-57188
ISBN 0-669-02371-X

Published simultaneously in Canada.

Printed in the United States of America.

International Standard Book Number: 0-669-02371-X

Library of Congress Catalog Card Number: 78-57188

To the living memory of my great teacher,
Martin Buber

Contents

Foreword   ix

Acknowledgments   xiii

Chapter 1   **The Kibbutz Movement**   1

             Origin, Variety, and Change   1
             References   17

Chapter 2   **Education in the Kibbutz**   19

             References   25

Chapter 3   **Women in the Kibbutz**   27

             How Did It Happen?   32
             Changing the Status Quo   37
             References   42

Chapter 4   **The Family in the Kibbutz**   45

             The Future of the Kibbutz Family   57
             References   65

Chapter 5   **Parents and Peers**   67

             Parents' Roles in Early Kibbutzim   68
             Parent-Child Relations in Today's Kibbutzim   71
             Early Research   79
             Parents and Peers—An Updated Research   82
             Spheres of Influence   87
             Quality of Relations   90
             Influence of Age, Sex, Familism   96
             Parents' Views   99
             References   102

Chapter 6   **Caregivers**   105

             Research on Metaplot   108
             Cooperation between Parents and Caregivers   113
             References   119

Chapter 7	**Epilogue**	121
	The Second Kibbutz Generation	121
	A Necessary Change	127
	References	129
Appendix	**Martin Buber and the Kibbutz Movement**	131
	References	133
	Index	135
	About the Author	·143

Foreword

For anyone interested in the potentialities and limits of human nature for the achievement of radical change in human social relations, utopian communities, created for the purpose of implementing a vision of society based on man's highest ideals of equality, justice, and humanity, constitute crucial experiments for study and analysis. It is all the more disappointing, therefore, that one of the characteristics of utopian communities is that they are short-lived, most of them coming to an end shortly after, if not during, the life-time of their founders. This in itself might perhaps suggest that the potentiality of human beings for implementing their ideals is much less impressive than their ability to conceive of them. Or at least we might have drawn this conclusion were it not for the fact that the kibbutz movement—the utopian movement in Israel—constitutes an important exception to the above generalization.

The first kibbutz was founded in 1910 with a few score members. Today, the kibbutz movement comprises two hundred-forty kibbutzim with one hundred thousand members. More important, although a minority of those born and raised in kibbutzim have since made their lives in the outside world, the majority have remained. Hence, older kibbutzim have witnessed not only their children, but also their grandchildren growing into adulthood as members, workers, and leaders. The kibbutz movement, moreover, has not only survived, but by almost any criterion one would use, it has achieved a creative survival. Comprising only three percent of Israel's population, its contributions to the economic, political, military, cultural, and artistic life of that country has been entirely disproportionate to its numbers. It is not surprising, therefore, that for many observers the creation of the kibbutz has been one of the signal achievements of Zionist history.

But the survival—even the creative survival—of the kibbutz movement is not the only (or even the most important) reason that it holds a special interest for the comparative study of society and culture. Since this movement was founded as an attempt to achieve a particular vision of a just society, and since this vision has now been handed down to the children and grandchildren of the founders, one of the important questions one wants to ask about the kibbutz movement is, what has happened to that attempt now that (to use the distinction of Karl Mannheim) the "utopia" of its founders has become the "ideology" of their descendants? To put it differently, to what extent have the successive generations of the kibbutz embraced the values of the founding generation and the institutions which they created for their realization? This is the major (though not the only) question which is addressed in this book with respect not to the totality of kibbutz values and institutions, but to those that are related to its revolution in the traditional systems of the family, socialization, and sex-role differentiation.

The author of this book is uniquely qualified to address this question. Unlike others of us who have written about the kibbutz, Dr. Gerson is not only a student of the kibbutz, but he is himself a founding member of one of the most successful (and beautiful) kibbutzim in Israel. A kibbutz member for forty-five years, as well as the long-time director of research into kibbutz education at Oranim, the kibbutz teachers' college, Gerson has studied kibbutz life from the perspective not only of an "objective" researcher, but also of a dedicated kibbutznick. This dual perspective (which he shared with some few other kibbutz scholars) confers special interest and importance upon his observations and interpretations. This is not to say, of course, that the views of "insiders" are closer to the truth than those of "outsiders"—in this country such a thesis has led, for example, to (in my view) the absurd belief of many colleges and universities that only blacks are qualified to teach black studies or that only women are qualified to teach women's studies. It is to say, however, that insiders often have different views from outsiders, and where this is the case, then, all things being equal, attention to both sets of views provides a closer approximation to the truth than is typically afforded by either taken alone.

The advantages of a researcher being an insider are obvious. The insider not only has access to information that is not available—or at least not readily available—to the outsider, but what is more important he can check his interpretations against not only his objective "data," but also his subjective "experience." The latter advantage, of course, is a double-edged sword. Since an insider has a commitment to the object of his study that an outsider, however sympathetic, can never have, his "subjective" stance introduces a potentiality for bias and distortion which is perhaps greater than that confronting the "objective" outsider. It is to Gerson's credit that this book shows little evidence of that kind of bias or distortion. Rather than depicting an idyllic society, he has painted a realistic portrait of the kibbutz, warts and all. This is not to say that Gerson writes as a detached observer. On the contrary, he writes as a partisan who, moreover, makes no attempt to conceal his partisanship. Thus, he leaves no doubt that he is *for* socialism, he is *for* progress, he is *for* feminism. Hence, in assessing, for example, the return to family sleeping arrangements in some kibbutzim, or the tendency of many kibbutz women to return to traditional feminine roles, he does not conceal the fact that his sharp criticisms of these trends and their proponents stem from his strong commitment to feminist values.

Since I do not share all of Gerson's values (but for other reasons as well), it is not surprising that I do not agree with all of his conclusions and interpretations. Nevertheless, I am happy to write the foreword to his book—indeed, it is a testimony to Gerson's openness as a scholar that, despite our important disagreements, he asked me to write the foreword—because I believe that it is a serious and valuable attempt to understand a movement that may just be the most important volunteeristic and democratic effort at radical social change in this century. This book is an important contribution to the ongoing dialogue concerning the characteristics of that movement and its implications for our understanding of human nature and society.

Melford E. Spiro
Professor of Anthropology
University of California

Acknowledgments

I wish to express my gratitude and deep appreciation to my friends and colleagues who helped me with the writing and publication of this book. First and foremost, I wish to express my gratitude to three American friends: Professor Israel Zwerling, Professor Melford Spiro, and Charles Silberman. Their comments, encouragement, and ceaseless efforts to promote this book have been of decisive importance to me.

I wish to thank Stella Stattman (Bar Ilan University) whose profound knowledge of English contributed a great deal to the style of the manuscript. My colleagues at the Institute of Research on Kibbutz Education, Oranim (now part of the Institute for Research and Study of the Kibbutz, Haifa University), greatly helped my work. I am particularly indebted to Michael Nathan who offered his help in order to give the manuscript a more concise form. He as well as other colleagues—especially Zvi Lavi, Professor Shmuel Nagler, and Moni Alon—contributed a great deal by their remarks and suggestions concerning various chapters.

Rivka Peeri, the secretary of the Institute, facilitated my work all along, both with her infinite devotion to the task in hand and with her organizational talents.

Last but not least, I want to thank my wife Chava who stood by me during all the arduous stages of writing and publishing this book.

May 1978   *Menachem Gerson*
                                             Kibbutz Hazorea

1

The Kibbutz Movement

Origin, Variety, and Change

The great interest which the kibbutz has aroused in the last twenty years is reflected in the large number of articles and books that have appeared in many countries, particularly in the United States. Almost all the books, however, have been written by visitors who stayed in one specific kibbutz for periods ranging from seven weeks to twelve months; and their work is, of necessity, a record of the impressions of an outsider. Because such a record is based on limited experience and was compiled during a limited period of time, the picture which it presents is generalized and static. A historical perspective, an awareness of change within the kibbutz movement in response to changes in Israeli society or to world events, recognition of the differences both between individual kibbutzim and between the various federations of kibbutzim—all these are denied to the visitor. This book is an attempt to write about the kibbutz from the inside, from the perspective of one who has lived for forty-five years as a member of a kibbutz. Both the observer from outside and the participant/observer inside apply their own set of values to all they see and experience. But if both are aware of their biases, the difference between them lies not in their degree of objectivity but in the degree of familiarity with the concepts, the ideology, the aspirations, and, above all, the problems of day-to-day living. In all these, the knowledge of the insider is bound to be more intimate and complete. He does not see the kibbutz as a uniform mode of settlement which has always operated according to fixed social, economic, and political guidelines. He knows that each kibbutz is different from another kibbutz, even if they are both members of the same federation, and that each is a multifaceted unit, constantly evolving and changing. And he knows from his own experience that it is one thing to make ideological declarations and quite a different matter to realize their principles in daily life. Yet he also knows that the constant attempt to do so is the very essence of kibbutz living.

We shall use this introductory chapter to present the reader with a description of the formative years of two early kibbutzim which served as prototypes for their respective federations and to give a brief account of the history and composition of the three main kibbutz federations. Such an account will help to explain one reason for variety within the kibbutz movement, namely, that which stems from affiliation to one or other of the kibbutz federations. There are, however, other factors which make for differences between individual kibbutzim

1

and which are worthy of brief mention. The cultural origin of members in any given kibbutz influences the level of education, the degree of political awareness, the type of cultural life and possibly even the climate of interpersonal relations. Size, age, geographical location, and the measure of economic success also play their part in creating differences. Where the kibbutz has been established for many years, the measure of influence of the second and third generations will be greater than that found in younger kibbutzim. A border settlement will suffer a great level of stress in times of political or military tension. Lastly, the measure of economic success affects both internal and external relationships. A successful kibbutz may even face some of the problems of an affluent society such as squander.

But whatever the origin of its members, the size, age, location, or measure of success of any kibbutz, whatever its affiliation to one of the federations, certain fundamental principles guide its operation. It will be helpful to briefly review these principles here.

The kibbutz is a socialist community. In accordance with the highest principles of social justice, the kibbutz manages its affairs by direct, democratic control. The social responsibility of the individual and the voluntary nature of the organization are sufficient to ensure a high level of social order without the need for a police force or courts to impose control from outside. Nor is there a permanent governing body. The means of production are collectively owned and are operated by the labor force of the kibbutz[a] according to a plan of production and consumption which is worked out every year by the economic committee of the kibbutz. Of necessity, in order to ensure the smooth operation of a planned economy, there has to be an assignment of duties in both production and service areas. This assignment is determined by communal bodies whose members are not permanent officials but are elected for periods of two to three years by the general assembly, which meets weekly.

In accordance with socialist principles, all forms of work are of equal value in the eyes of the kibbutz member. It follows, then, that no distinction is made in the standard of living of a member on the basis of the work in which he is engaged. The needs of all members—food, housing, education, culture, health services, geriatric care—are provided in equal measure to all by the community. The upbringing of all children until the age of eighteen is the responsibility of the kibbutz community as a whole.

Because the kibbutz regards itself not as an isolated social unit but rather as an active participant in the social and political life of Israel, it safeguards its involvement organizationally by the formal obligation of every kibbutz to put a certain proportion of its members (about 5 percent) at the disposal of the

---

[a]The main exception to this principle, an exception officially accepted by the federations of kibbutzim, is in the building trade. Since there is a permanent shortage of workers in the dynamic kibbutz economy, a countrywide organization to carry out building work was established.

federations on whose behalf they carry out duties in all spheres of Israeli public life—in politics, education, economics, immigrant absorption, youth movement work, etc.

The realization of the basic principles of kibbutz living has had far-reaching results. In the economic sphere, it has contributed greatly to the high degree of economic efficiency and success which marks many kibbutzim. In the social sphere, it has minimized the dependence of the individual on a ruling and self-perpetuating bureaucracy and accorded him respect and status whatever his physical and mental powers. In the realm of Israeli public life, the impact of kibbutz involvement and the dissemination of its values have greatly influenced the shape of the government and the form of its services, an influence far in excess of the numerical strength of the kibbutz movement.[b]

Without the constant striving to realize the principles of social justice, a striving which is the very essence of kibbutz living, it is doubtful if the kibbutz could ensure its existence. After all, this small socialist cell within a capitalist society now comprises a mere 3.4 percent of the total population. The impact of the kibbutz movement on Israeli life is thus a reflection of the character of the members and their persistent struggle toward the fulfillment of their ideals. We use the word *struggle* for although it is easy to make radical theoretical declarations, it is quite another matter to realize the principles in a harsh and frequently adverse reality. No reasonable human being can expect a perfect realization of the principles which guide kibbutz living. The most a human being who chooses this way of life can demand of himself is that he does his utmost to strive toward the realization of these principles and that his criticism of reality is based on values laid down by the kibbutz movement. The confrontation between elevated principles and everyday realities in kibbutz living will be one of our concerns.

What prompted the establishment of the early kibbutzim? What were the principles and the reality which gave them birth?

Origin of the Kibbutzim

Degania, the first kvutza, was founded in 1910. At that time, the number of Jews living in Palestine was about 70,000, two-thirds of whom were orthodox Jews living on charity while the remaining third, members of the first Zionist immigration wave, had become landowners, employers of Arab labor. The country was barren and desolate, and living conditions were harsh and primitive. Outside the small urban centers of Jewish life, a settler found himself in a hostile Arab environment, desperately alone and isolated. It was to this world that the

---

[b]While we regard the recent victory of the Begin coalition as a fundamental change in Israel's policy and social structure, it is too early to determine its influence on the position of the kibbutz in Israel.

young pioneers who were to found Degania came.[1] They arrived with the Second Aliyah, an immigration wave whose members were imbued with ideas of social justice as an integral part of the Zionist effort to resettle the homeland. For this group, two tasks were clear and compelling—adaptation to hard, physical labor and the opening of large areas of wasteland, previously inaccessible, to Jewish settlements. In September 1911, twelve young Russian Jews recently immigrated, including two women, erected their first buildings in the exhausting heat of the Jordan Valley.

Their decision to work together was an act of collective genius, generated by the cultural background of the members and the effect on them of the harsh conditions of their new life. There were members imbued with Russian ideas of social revolution who saw their struggle in Palestine as part of a similar aspiration for a better society. There were those who compared the new way of life with that of the Essenes, seeing in it the beginnings of a new utopia. But, above all, for all of them, there was the need to find an answer to the difficulties involved in adaptation to the low standard of living, to hard, physical labor in a cruel climate, and to separation from the warmth and support of their families. In one way or another, the members of the group, disturbed by the hardships of working as hired laborers and of social isolation, came to see the establishment of a voluntary, collective community as the only way of fulfilling the Zionist, socialist dream.

Yet although the decision to work collectively was made, for many years collectivism existed only in work and kitchen duties. Expenses for clothing and cultural activities were borne by members separately. It took a number of years before increasing membership and maturation of ideas led to complete collectivism.

In 1919, Joseph Bussel, the leader of the group, put forward a plan for the development of Degania designed to accommodate 25 workers, both men and women. Implicit in it was the assumption that Degania would be a permanent place of settlement for a permanent group. After the first fourteen years of Degania's existence, it had 43 permanent members, but 365 others had worked there for short periods and decided to leave, among them 23 who had been accepted as full members. Many reasons were given for the fluctuation in numbers. Some members complained about the difficulties of this way of life. Some were attracted to a more individualistic and family-oriented way of life and left to settle in a cooperative, small-holder type of settlement (the moshav), of which Nahalal is an early and representative example. Others gave a more ideological explanation for their decision to leave Degania: they argued that it was the duty of the *chalutz*, the pioneer, to be on the move constantly in order to establish more and more settlements and to cultivate increasing areas of desolate land. Whatever the reason given, it seems clear that the decisive factor which caused the large turnover of members was not reasons of principle but rather personal motives, mainly the inability to adjust to hard conditions and the lack of family life in the group.[2] Almost all the founder members were bachelors. It was not that women were not attracted to this way of life, but simply that the difficulty of their physical adaptation to the conditions and the impossibility of obtaining outside employment in the early years proved too great an obstacle. It is no wonder that the young pioneers began to question the possibility of ever enjoying a family life in what was a frontier outpost and to wonder whether, in fact, they could even forge a permanent way of life out of the unique venture.

In addition to the struggle with their own personal problems, the young pioneers had to face the discouraging attitude of official bodies. But most of the founding members and an increasing number of young pioneers coming after them rejected the adventurous approach which called for constant movement from the establishment of one new outpost to the other and felt the need for perseverance in one place. It was this obstinate spirit of day-to-day realization of an ideal which built Degania—and after Degania, the whole kibbutz movement.

In 1924, twelve years after the establishment of Degania, a new settlement was founded at Beth Alpha in the Valley of Jesreel. Its founders came in the wake of the Balfour declaration, fired with the desire to implement radical social change, as promised by the Russian revolution. The newcomers came to a land in which they could rely only on their own sense of purpose to maintain their enthusiasm and dynamism and to save them from being absorbed into the existing framework or from leaving the country in disillusionment.

The nucleus of the group that was to found Beth Alpha came to Israel as members of *HaShomer Hatzair*, the first and most influential of the Zionist youth movements of the Diaspora. After their immigration to Israel, some of the members of the movement, a small elite group, settled at Betania. This was an "encounter group" of enthusiastic youth, immersed in its own group life, seeking the abolition of boundaries between individuals through confessions made at enchanted nights before the whole group. Their main ideal was the creation of truly communal relations between members of the group, and this they pursued with an almost religious zeal. To them, the enthusiasm and intimacy of the Betania group were a true realization of the values of their youth movement. In spite of their ideals, however, they succumbed quite soon to the built-in conflicts that an exclusive body of this type engenders. In addition, members began to feel that their kind of group could not provide the answers to the problems encountered by other movement members scattered throughout Palestine. Relations with their charismatic leader became so strained that he had to leave the group.[c] The members of the group came to regard the elitist character of their small unit as a burden and a hindrance; therefore, they joined forces with a less

---

[c]It is worth noting that in contrast to many utopian communities, since that time the kibbutz has never had a charismatic leader, even though some had fulfilled this role in the youth movement in the Gola. It seems that the egalitarian and task-oriented character of the kibbutz does not allow for charismatic leadership.

selective group of HaShomer Hatzair members in order to establish the first kibbutz of this movement. The idea was not new. As early as 1922, they had conceived the notion of establishing a network of autonomous agricultural kibbutzim[3] to absorb the members of the HaShomer Hatzair movement who were still in Europe and to perpetuate its aims, in particular to give members the opportunity for the full growth of the personality.[4] It is a sign of the strength of the movement that nine months after its establishment, Beth Alpha already had 102 members, 26 of them women.

In many ways, the beginnings of both Degania and Beth Alpha were similar. The members of both kibbutzim shared the Zionist pioneering approach to work and to the land of Israel. The members of both groups faced similar problems of adjustment in the transition to physical labor in a cruel climate and to a collective way of life. But whereas the founders of Degania sought in the kibbutz a solution to pressing economic and social conditions, the settlers of Beth Alpha were seeking the realization of their ideological aims as well. As a result, in the immediate sphere, the frustrations and frictions which are inevitably generated when people live in close proximity were felt particularly keenly by the Beth Alpha group, while in the larger sphere the desire to practice their social ideals caused the activity of its members to be extended even at the earliest stages into the public and political life of Israel.

Both Degania and Beth Alpha were the prototypes for two of the three kibbutz federations which were to develop later. The importance of federative organization for the success of the kibbutz has been explained by Martin Buber in his penetrating study *Paths in Utopia*.[5] Here Buber analyzes in great detail the failure of the various utopian communities and describes the kibbutz as the only one which did not fail. As one of the reasons for this "exemplary non-failure," Buber mentions the fact that the kibbutzim created a federative organization as distinct from the other utopian settlements which remained isolated units. The federalization, that is, "the alliance under the same principle which regulates the internal structure"[6] of the units, is the force which, according to Buber, enabled the kibbutz movement to exert an educative influence on the surrounding society. In Buber's opinion,[d] without this radiating of its values on society as a whole, a socialist (or religious) settlement does not fulfill its task.

Buber's contention will become clearer after we describe the character of the three main kibbutz federations. We have omitted the fourth kibbutz movement, the religious kibbutz movement, but not because we believe that its relative smallness (13 kibbutzim among the 241 kibbutzim in existence today in Israel) renders it insignificant. On the contrary, the integration of Jewish tradition and kibbutz life to which it aspires attracts people of great worth who are capable of resolving the conflicts made by the demands of two quite divergent value systems. But the religious kibbutz has very special problems to face and is

---

[d]On Buber's relation to the kibbutz movement, see the Appendix.

less involved in the free interchange of opinions which cooperation in many constructive ventures engenders within the three large kibbutz federations. The special character of the religious kibbutz thus makes it difficult to include in this discussion.

Nevertheless, there is one fundamental element which is common to all four kibbutz federations. This is what the Hebrew language calls *chalutziut*.[e] In common usage, this term denotes the attitude of the first generation of settlers to their mission in Palestine. But, according to its linguistic origin, it also implies a pioneering approach to life. The very opposite of the chalutz is the self-centered individual, totally absorbed and content with his private ambitions and interests, with his own career and family; the chalutz is ready for lifelong service to an ideal which is greater than his private life.[7] If this view is considered, it is easy to understand why a religious approach has often been ascribed to these atheistic chalutzim—religion to be interpreted as Buber understands it, not as traditional orthodoxy.

Three Kibbutz Federations

We have spoken generally of the differences among kibbutzim and have referred to differences among the kibbutz federations.[f] The time has now come for us to make these differences clearer through a description of the origins and form of the three large kibbutz federations. We shall start with the earliest one, Ichud HaKvutzot VeHaKibbutzim[8] (literally, the Union of Collective Settlements), in short, Ichud.

The first settlement in this federation was Degania. The early settlers had originally regarded a small unit of 25 families as ideal, feeling that such a compact group could best safeguard the status of the individual member and allow him to become involved in all aspects of kibbutz life. When, however, in the early 1930s members of the youth movement Gordonia decided to join the federation, the old policy became the target of criticism. It was contended that such a limited group encouraged parochialism and failed to utilize the economic potential of the kvutza to the full. Under the leadership of Pinchas Lubianiker (Lavon) the members of Gordonia succeeded in effecting a change of policy. It was decided that every kvutza was to be allowed to decide its size but that central authorities were to voice their opinion on the economic and social potential of each group. It was understood that without a central organization, there was no possibility of realizing goals which were common to a number of groups.

---

[e]The *chalutz* is a member of a vanguard. For the linguistic origin of this word, see Numbers 32: 20-32.

[f]HaShomer Hatzair is the youth movement from which kibbutz Artzi has grown. Gordonia is one of the movements of which Ichud Hakibbutzim Vehakvutzot is composed.

It was during the deliberations on the affiliation of Gordonia to the older settlements that a clear demarcation line was drawn between the principles which were to characterize the new union and those of the other two kibbutz movements, in particular concerning limitation of size and the exclusive emphasis on agriculture.

Hever HaKvutzot, and later Ichud, always belonged to Mapai, the moderate socialist party which has been responsible for policy in Israel even before the inception of the state. Thus, there was no need to include politics in the activities of the federation. As it was, quite a few of its members held central positions in the government. The other two kibbutz federations were shaken by deep ideological crises arising from party politics and from the controversial attitude toward the Soviet Union. The members of Ichud, identifying as they do with the political establishment of the country, have been spared these crises. On the other hand, the close connection with the government seems to have reduced the strength of the conception of the kibbutz as "the other society" which is bound to follow its specific rules. The difference in self-perception has been evinced in the attitude to hired labor which has been much more employed in the Ichud than in the other federations.

The second kibbutz federation we shall describe is *Hakibbutz Hameuchad* (the United Kibbutz Movement). This group of kibbutzim had its origins in the *G'dud HaAvoda*, the Labor Brigade,[9] to use the name given by Y. Trumpeldor. The members of the Labor Brigade arrived in the wake of the Third Aliyah (mass immigration wave).

Their social philosophy was deeply influenced by the Russian Revolution of 1917, by its elan and enthusiasm, by its faith in the realization of revolutionary aims in one great upheaval, and by its belief that the great day of revolution was at hand and that its all-important aim was the construction of a new social system, which was not to be impeded by considerations such as individual self-fulfillment. The Labor Brigade defined its aim as "the upbuilding of the country through an all-embracing commune of the Jewish workers in Palestine." The Brigade opposed selectivity in the recruitment of members; it wanted to include an unlimited and steadily growing number of individuals and small groups. Its ideal was a kind of Red Army for the purposes of colonization in Palestine, which was to be organized in one large central organization. It was suggested that all members and groups should pool their wages and thus ensure equality of living conditions among all the groups of the Labor Brigade. Its members would be directed by the central committee to work wherever there was a national need; and, as a matter of fact, the members of the Brigade shouldered the heaviest tasks and undertook the most dangerous assignments. In all groups of the Brigade scattered all over the country, fierce discussions were conducted centering, in the main, on the compatibility of socialism and Zionism and on the future of the Jewish people. They contributed in no small measure to the messianic atmosphere typical of every gathering of Brigade members. Unfortunately, the revolutionary ideas of an all-embracing community of Jewish workers ran counter to the social differentiation between skilled and unskilled workers which had developed in Palestine in the 1920s. Thus, while part of the Brigade founded their first kibbutz at Ein Charod (1921), a leftist part of the Brigade became gradually more disillusioned about the possibility of constructive socialism in Palestine. After Trumpeldor's death, Elkind, the revered leader of the Brigade, declared that a commune could not exist in a capitalist country but only in the Soviet Union. His next step was the only logical one. In 1928, together with 40 other members of the Brigade, he left the country and established a Jewish commune in the Crimea.[g]

Ein Charod, the first and most prominent of the kibbutzim of Hakibbutz Hameuchad to be founded by the Brigade, did not long retain its allegiance. Guided by Yizchak Tabenkin, the recognized leader of this kibbutz movement, the members realized that a permanent settlement could not be established as long as members could be directed by the executive of the Labor Brigade to serve in other places. As a result, Ein Harod decided to sever its connection with the Brigade.

Yet, in spite of these differences in opinion, kibbutz Meuchad was deeply influenced by the approach of the Brigade. To Tabenkin,[10] *chalutziut* was a means for the realization of the Jewish national and social revolution. Hence, it is not surprising to find that the ideology of this movement is based on the following principles:

The kibbutz should be a large settlement with no predetermined limit to the number of members.

It should be open to all comers and not restricted to members of a particular youth movement.

It should engage in all forms of essential production, both agricultural and industrial, as a way of achieving economic success and as a means of fulfilling national tasks.

It should maintain a centralistic organization to prevent kibbutz egoism and social disintegration.

At all times its members have to be ready to devote themselves entirely to the national needs of the moment.

A tendency to play down the importance of political or social theory resulted from this approach to the demands of the nation while a more emotional and volitional approach was encouraged.

---

[g]Elkind was later executed during one of the Stalinist purges.

These lofty principles have extorted a high prices from Kibbutz Meuchad. Absolute demands from individuals who were not prepared for kibbutz life have resulted in a high dropout rate of people from the kibbutz. In 1951, the disregard for an explicit, common political ideology brought about a split on political grounds within the movement. This split caused the once largest kibbutz federation to be relegated to the place of the smallest of the three federations. On the other hand, the empiricism of Kibbutz Meuchad allowed it to recognize much earlier than Kibbutz Artzi, the third and more left-wing movement, the true character of Soviet communism and thus to ward off the deep ideological crisis which befell its sister movement.

Whatever one's attitude to the principles of and organization within Kibbutz Meuchad, the willingness of the members to undertake the most arduous tasks in colonization and in national defense cannot be questioned.

The third kibbutz federation is the Kibbutz Artzi[h] of HaShomer Hatzair, the youth movement which founded Beth Alpha. In 1927, five years after the foundation of Beth Alpha, a countrywide federation was set up on the basis of an all-embracing ideological program. It expressed the firm ideological orientation of the founder generation. It goes quite contrary to the empirical orientation which prevails both in the other kibbutz federations and in the Labor Party as well.[11] This orientation of Kibbutz Artzi was apparently the lever which lifted this movement out of early esoteric inclinations. The 1927 program aimed toward a synthesis of Zionism and revolutionary socialism. The cardinal importance of Jewish-Arab understanding was early recognized. Kibbutz Artzi sees the kibbutz as an instrument for the realization of Zionism and for supporting the struggle of the working class. Yet it also regards the kibbutz as an end in itself, a prototype of the future communist society, which strives toward the integration of the individual with his community. For the sake of a communal way of life, the kibbutz creates conditions for the unrestricted development of the individual; it establishes a new social ethic and strives toward a solution to the problems of the family, of women, and of child education.

In spite of the autonomy granted to each kibbutz in its social and economic affairs, the movement has recognized the need for a strong central body and inspired leadership. For many years, this has been provided by Meir Yaari and Yaakov Chasan, working in close cooperation with each other.

This federation strives to develop a common outlook on life that unites all its members (with a rather unfortunate term—it was called *ideological collectivism*). The struggle toward this consensus has made Kibbutz Artzi the most highly principled as well as the strongest and best organized of the kibbutz federations. At the same time, in some areas it has stifled mental awareness and growth. It occasionally happened, for example, that the central authorities of Kibbutz Artzi were more interested in the "right" decision taken by kibbutz

---

[h]*Artzi* means countrywide.

representatives than in the process of clarification itself. The result was quite often an orthodox or closed-minded[12] approach which did not take into consideration the vital importance of dissent as a stimulus for alertness. Similarly, because leanings toward Soviet Russia were always very strong even with the reservations created by Russia's anti-Zionist attitude and dismissal of the kibbutz, it took a long time before the antidemocratic nature of the Soviet government was fully acknowledged. The tensions inside Kibbutz Artzi reached their climax when the second kibbutz-born generation activated itself in the kibbutzim.

The highly principled approach of this closely knit movement has created problems in the political sphere too. When Kibbutz Artzi decided to form a political party (Mapam), together with other nonkibbutz groups, practical political problems became a source of contention within the kibbutz movement, especially on the question of whether Mapam should remain an autonomous party or align itself with the Israel Labor Party.

There are many people who believe that the differences among the three kibbutz federations belong to the past and are therefore devoid of significance in the present. They argue that most of the differences have disappeared in the second kibbutz generation. The heated discussions which were once held about the optimal size of a kibbutz have little meaning today. Most kibbutzim are quite large, and the few which remain small did not do so from choice. The debate on pure agriculture as against the inclusion of industry has been terminated in favor of the latter. A striving for a commonly held political view in fact exists in all three movements but is less stringent than it used to be. The differences in the educational level which existed in the past have disappeared in the second kibbutz generation, all of whom enjoy the same opportunities for personal development (through education of all kibbutz-born children up to the age of 18) and all of whom undergo the same experiences during military service.

Although ostensibly differences among the three movements may be less readily distinguishable, we believe that they are still felt in many aspects of life. Traces of past tendencies are still very much present. The central authorities in the Ichud still exercise less influence in the individual kibbutz than the authorities of the sister movements. Kibbutz Artzi still places strong emphasis on ideological clarification by the group as a whole. In Kibbutz Meuchad, stress is still laid on the contribution of the kibbutz to the nation rather than on its contribution to a new solution to the problems of human relations by virtue of its very existence. Yet, since both Ichud and Kibbutz Meuchad are affiliated to the Labor Party, negotiations between them are now under way in order to reach unification.

Whatever the answer to the present-day significance of historical differences among the three kibbutz federations may be, the fact is that they have achieved a large measure of cooperation. This is due to the difficulties and problems the whole kibbutz movement had to face after the foundation of the state of Israel.

Changes in the Kibbutzim

With the foundation of the state of Israel in 1948, the kibbutz movement found that it no longer attracted a considerable proportion of the newcomers to Israel. Its numerical peak was reached at the beginning of 1948 when it comprised 7.8 percent of the total population. In 1951, after the first wave of mass immigration, the parallel figure was only 6 percent. During these three years, the Jewish population of Israel had grown by 96 percent while the kibbutz population had increased by only 27.5 percent.[13] The establishment of the state brought a new type of immigrant to Israel and for a short time even caused the role of the kibbutz to be questioned.[14]

The new mass immigration was conspicuous in that it was not comprised of young people who had decided to immigrate to Israel on the strength of their adherence to their chalutzic values; in the main, they were Jews who had recently escaped from the holocaust in Europe or Jews from Arab countries who wanted to escape growing persecution. Once in Israel, most of these people tried to unite with the rest of their families as soon as possible. Many of them were old people or young children. Neither the immigrant from Europe nor the one from the East was attracted to the kibbutz. Physical labor was regarded by both groups as demeaning, the occupation of the lowest levels of society. For the Europeans, the protective wire fence around the kibbutz and the simple menu, without choice of dishes, reminded them of their past in Nazi concentration camps, while immigrants from Arab countries far removed from modern culture could not understand the kibbutz with its rejection of a patriarchal society and its system of communal education. In addition, the position and prestige of the kibbutz changed after the foundation of the state. The system of voluntary service, so important for Israel's growth until then, seemed out of date, an anachronism and incongruous, in the newly achieved workings of governmental apparatus. Until then, the kibbutz had been recognized by most Israelis as a highly appreciated elite group; now a new elite was proclaimed by the leaders of the state. The members of this elite were the efficient state official, the officer in Israel's army, the technical expert—all of them so much needed by the new state struggling for its existence. Ben-Gurion attacked the kibbutz movement for what he considered a lack of chalutzic spirit and for its orthodoxy, both of which prevented the kibbutz movement from absorbing great numbers of immigrants as hired laborers at a time when abject living conditions and unemployment were the lot of so many of them. The split on political grounds which in 1951 befell the then largest kibbutz federation, Kibbutz Meuchad, seemed to illustrate a widespread feeling that with the foundation of the state of Israel the kibbutz no longer had a significant role to play in the development of the country.

In order to retain its place in Israeli society, the kibbutz movement had to adapt itself to the new situation created by the establishment of the state. As Israeli society grew in numbers and diversity, the kibbutz unit became larger and more complex. As the state developed and new markets opened both within and without Israel, the kibbutz responded by increasing or changing agricultural produce and by setting up industries. So successful has the response of the kibbutz been to the changing size and form of Israeli society that the average net income of the kibbutzim has been raised into the upper third bracket of Israel's population, based on real net income.[15] An adequate standard of living has become a striking feature of the kibbutz of the 1970s. The rise in the standard of living is reflected in the greater diversification allowed in private consumption, in the quality and variety of durable goods, and in the fashionable clothing. The improvements in the quality of life extend beyond the individual and his private dwelling and are expressed in many ways in the kibbutz, in the size and quality of the buildings, and in particular in the beautiful landscaping in which many kibbutzim excel.[i]

There have been other changes. The larger membership of the kibbutz as well as the greater complexity and sophistication of life in the kibbutz has made it impossible for every single problem to be brought up at the highest decision-making level, at the weekly assembly. Thus many decisions have to be made by the various elected committees. They sometimes feel the need to introduce fixed statutes (to be approved by the assembly) and in this way to alleviate the difficulty of making decisions on matters which are often of great concern to the individual. Of course, even in this process of growing institutionalization, an appeal to the assembly is always open to the individual. The degree to which generalizing measures are taken varies in different kibbutzim.

The stronger the human relations in a kibbutz and the greater the measure of individual identification with the community, the less rigid it is in its codification of behavior. With the rising importance of the family in the kibbutz, the admittance of new members has become more lenient than it used to be, even in those federations which once demanded rigorous selection of potential members. A new candidate is frequently accepted simply on the strength of marriage to an accepted member, with the understanding that he will prove himself reliable in both work and social behavior. The importance of affiliation on ideological grounds is receding more and more in these deliberations. Small wonder that under these conditions every kibbutz has a periphery of members who are not active in decision making in the assembly, in committee work, or in political work. The relative size and influence of this periphery vary from kibbutz to kibbutz.

A further differentiation concerning the social appreciation of work is coming into being. The original formula of "every type of work has equal value" has become too simple a statement. It was valid for the founder generation who,

---

[i]Here, too, individual differences among kibbutzim reveal themselves. The extent of the landscaping carried out in the kibbutz depends both on the allocation of workforce for this work and on the activity of the individual family. Thus the extent and beauty of the gardens are an immediate indication of the attitude of a kibbutz to its members, and vice versa.

with great effort, had to acquire the ability to do physical work efficiently and who found enormous satisfaction in the creation of a new society. Such a situation no longer exists for the second and third kibbutz generation who acquire the ability for heavy physical work from early childhood "naturally" and excel in it to a degree which is often surprising to a veteran member who came originally from the Diaspora. For these later generations, the new society is an existing fact, and they feel perfectly at home in it. It is no wonder, then, that the kibbutz-born generation looks elsewhere for its self-realization; in particular, they turn to permanent and skilled jobs. The growing industrialization of the kibbutz meets their needs and turns it from a subjective need into an economic asset. This development does not express a preference for intellectual or white-collar work as some outside observers assume. Appreciation of physical work is as great today as it ever was. One of the reasons for this high regard for physical work seems to have a psychological origin. Under kibbutz conditions, physical work demands much involvement with coworkers and a feeling of belonging, both of which provide a sense of basic security to the kibbutz member, even though the great density of life often makes for personal friction.

While economic conditions as well as the needs of the second kibbutz generation for self-fulfillment make the permanent job an accepted fact (as opposed to the job rotation as a means of safeguarding equality, as was practiced in the early days of the kibbutz), the principle of rotation is maintained as far as the distribution of administrative positions in the kibbutz is concerned. This principle of rotation of offices which entail decision making on the concerns of members is essential for a voluntary community such as the kibbutz. A feeling of permanent dependence on a few individuals would most severely damage the individual's ability to identify with the kibbutz.

A cardinal factor leading to many of the changes we have mentioned has been the rapid growth of industries in the kibbutz. Today there is a balance in the assignment of workers to agriculture and industry. It may soon turn in favor of industry because its average earning power is higher than that of agriculture. This combination of highly mechanized agriculture and industry has long since dispelled any of the doubts which were raised in the early days concerning the viability of the kibbutz as a socialist village.

As with any dynamic society, so in the kibbutz there has always been discussion on which values, beliefs, and institutions are basic to its organization and which can be changed without altering its fundamental character. Whatever form these ideological debates have taken in the kibbutz movement, there has never been any controversy on the need to eliminate all forms of social coercion or on the common responsibility of all members for the children. Nor has there ever been discord on the need for collective ownership of the means of production.

Collective ownership of the means of production serves a double purpose. It not only provides an agreed, efficient solution to an economic need but also fulfills an important social role in creating a new psychological approach to life within a kibbutz member. He learns that constant striving for personal gain and private economic success is no longer needed to give him security and status. Instead, he develops a sense of belonging and security by integration into the kibbutz community, by its acceptance of him as a valued member, and in the knowledge that the kibbutz as a whole considers itself responsible for his welfare.

We have already hinted at some of the changes which have been implemented in the kibbutz movement in response to changing conditions in Israel, and it is to the credit of the movement that they have taken place. I, personally, believe that to date there are only four problems whose resolution could involve changes which may constitute a threat to the kibbutz in its essential form. These are familistic trends, the problem of the fulfillment of women in the kibbutz, trends toward political isolation and the employment of hired labor. Except for the last one mentioned, they will be dealt with in the coming chapters.

There is a widespread misconception about change in the kibbutz which needs correction. The kibbutz is often presented as a movement which had its origin in lofty values but which deteriorated when faced with the problems of an adverse reality. This simple model does not allow for a historical interpretation of kibbutz development. Nor is it compatible with an objective understanding of change in the kibbutz. Inevitably, it leads to a conceptualization of "original highlights and decline," instead of the discernment of different stages in the development of the kibbutz (brought about mainly as a response to changes in Israeli society), each stage with its own achievements and hazards, each struggling for the realization of the basic kibbutz values. The simplistic method of evaluating change in the kibbutz takes the earliest stage of kibbutz development both as the ideal and as the yardstick against which the later stages are measured and arrives at the conclusion that the original values have been "betrayed." In a refined form, one can find this method of approach even in one of the earliest and most outstanding observers of the kibbutz, sociologist Yonina Talmon. She maintains[16] that in the early stages of kibbutz life, one of the prevailing values was a secular asceticism of the kind Max Weber saw as one of the fundamental tenets of Protestantism, namely, a deep contempt for creature comforts and material possessions.

If this sort of secular asceticism was, indeed, one of the fundamental values of the early days of the kibbutz, and if later on this attitude was replaced by the endeavor to achieve better living conditions, the conclusion seems obvious. At its early stage, it is argued, the kibbutz embodied the lofty ideals which had led to its establishment; but afterward a decline set in, and the previous values were betrayed. If this were true, it would clearly exemplify the model of change in the kibbutz which we are criticizing here. But is it true? Talmon is correct when she says that the economic goal of the early stage was consolidation of a productive economy; but the aim was not profit or high consumption, but preparation of additional resources. This has little to do with asceticism. Every form of socialism experiences a stage in which production has to be furthered by holding down consumption to a low level. But this does not mean that socialism does not regard raising the workers' standard of living as one of its cardinal aims. It is one thing to endorse the value of poverty as a permanent life-style because it promises salvation in heaven or because it contributes to the mortification of members, as in monastic societies or communes. It is quite another matter to accept poverty as a necessary corollary to hard conditions which will be changed in the course of time. Socialist thought has certainly no reason to idealize hardship. To the best of our knowledge and personal experience, kibbutz members have never taken a vow of poverty as, for instance, Spiro assumes.[17] In the sphere we are discussing here, no justification can be found for the interpretation of change in the kibbutz as a decline and betrayal of principles. Of course, the arduous test of poverty imposed upon members in the early years after the establishment of a kibbutz, which even today recurs in newly founded kibbutzim, no longer exists in a well-established kibbutz. There is no doubt that in the new situation different problems arise. Solidarity among members, for example, has to be achieved in new ways which are more complex than those created by the dictate of poverty. We can only repeat that every stage in the development of a kibbutz has its own achievements and its own dangers, its own responses and its own solutions. But there is no justification for branding every change for the better in the life of the kibbutz member as a decline.

While the kibbutz shares with the commune a sense of being an exemplary form of life, the kibbutz has never felt the need to isolate itself from external influences in order to zealously preserve its character.[18] The kibbutz has always considered itself an integral part of Israeli society, a part which has an important role to play in the national revival. In its desire to influence the structure of Israeli society, the kibbutz has turned its eyes outward, seeking political allies outside its own ranks. Unlike the commune, which rigidly opposed change, the kibbutz has always been aware of the need for changes in response to the changing conditions and demands of Israeli society. The changes which it has introduced into its structure have been made both to aid its own growth and development and to contribute in the best possible way to the needs of the Israeli scene. It is this willingness to change according to circumstances and specific needs which has helped the kibbutz to achieve permanence.

The value of the kibbutz to both the nation and the individual member rests primarily on a combination of three factors—the fulfillment of a national need, the striving for a new form of communal life, and regard for the needs of the individual member. In the first case, the need for colonization of barren regions of land and for inhabited areas along the borders demanded a permanent form of settlement. This task was willingly shouldered by the kibbutz movement which saw in it not only a way of responding to the demands of the moment but also a means of establishing a socialist society to be founded "here and now"

(Buber). It is this combination of elements which essentially distinguishes the kibbutz from the commune. The late Eliezer Hacohen, an eminent social philosopher of the kibbutz movement and one of the founders of Beth Alpha, has rightly said that the utopian communes have remained an ephemeral phenomenon, because they aimed only at self-improvement and did not aspire to change in society as a whole.[19]

In Arthur Ruppin's account of the history of Zionist colonization,[20] the establishment of the kibbutz was simply an ultimate attempt at settling young people on the land. Since the Zionist movement had no finances available to settle individuals and since all attempts to establish a system of small groups working under a trained administrator failed, the Zionist authorities had no option but to allow the young pioneers to try to cope in their own way. A far more balanced and accurate picture is given by Buber, who recognized a combination of elements in the decision to establish a communal way of life. In particular, Buber notes the strength of the idealism, of the sense of fulfilling both a personal desire and a national mission which impelled the early pioneers. Buber says[21]

The Jewish Village commune in Palestine owes its existence not to a doctrine but to a situation, to the needs, the stress, the demands of the situation. . . . This is certainly correct, but with one limitation. . . . What is called the ideology—I, personally, prefer the old but untarnished word "ideal"—was not just something to be added afterwards that would justify the accomplished facts. In the spirit of the members of the first Palestine communes, ideal motives joined hands with the dictates of the hour; and in the motives there was a curious mixture of memories of the Russian socialists, and the half-conscious aftereffects of the Bible's teachings about social justice. . . . There were various dreams about the future; people saw before them a new, more comprehensive form of the family, they saw themselves as the advance guard of the Worker's Movement, as the direct instrument for the realization of Socialism, as the prototype of the new society; they had as their goal the creation of a new man and a new world.

References

The letter H means that the book or paper is available only in Hebrew, even though its name appears here in English.

1. The description of Degania's beginnings is based mainly on *The Bussel Book* (Tel Aviv, 1960). Editor: S. Wurm, Tarbut Wehinuch. H.

2. Baratz, in *The Bussel Book*, p. 127. H.

3. *The Book of HaShomer Hatzair*, vol. 1 (Tel Aviv: Sifriat Poalim, 1956), pp. 85–90. H.

4. Elkana Margalit, *HaShomer Hatzair* (Tel Aviv: Hakibbutz Hameuchad Editing House, 1971). H.

5. Martin Buber, "An Experiment that Did Not Fail," *Paths in Utopia* (Boston: Beacon Press, 1971).

6. Ibid., p. 141.

7. Nathan Rotenstreich, *A People and Its State* (Tel Aviv: Hakibbutz Hameuchad Editing House, 1965), p. 236. H.

8. Cf. Baruch Ben-Avraham, *Chever HaKvutzot* (Tel Aviv: Am Oved, 1976). H. Chever Hakvutzot was the name of the two groups which united, as mentioned in the text; the name was changed to Ichud Hakvutzot Vehakibbutzim when the third group joined.

9. Cf. David Horowitz, *My Yesterday* (Tel Aviv: Shocken Edition, 1970), p. 179. H.

10. Our description is based mainly on a memorial to Tabenkin in "Mibifnim," the quarterly of Kibbutz Meuchad, July 1972, especially on an article by A. Tarschisch in this publication. H.

11. Berl Katznelson, the late veteran leader of Mapai, told me in a personal conversation many years ago, "When the two previous parties united and formed Mapai, I was appointed chairman of the Program Committee of the new party. I regard it as one of my merits that I have never convened this committee."

12. We use this term as it is used in M. Rokeach's book, *The Open and Closed Mind* (New York: Basic Books, 1960).

13. The figures mentioned are taken from Ben-Avraham's book.

14. Cf. Yonina Talmon Garber's paper, "The Position of Collective Settlements in Israel's Society," in *Individual and Society in the Kibbutz* (Jerusalem: Magnes Editing House, 1970). H.

15. Y. Shatil, *The Kibbutz: An Agricultural Village* (Spring Newsletter: Israeli Ministry of Agriculture, 1973).

16. Yonina Talmon, *Family and Community in the Kibbutz* (Cambridge, Mass.: Harvard University Press, 1972).

17. M. Spiro, *Kibbutz Venture in Utopia* (Cambridge, Mass.: Harvard University Press, 1956).

18. Rosabeth Moss Kanter, *Commitment and Community* (Cambridge, Mass.: Harvard University Press, 1972). In this book, Kanter mentions six commitment mechanisms which communes applied in order to guarantee their stability. The kibbutz has endorsed only two of them—investment and communion, in her terms.

19. Eliezer Hacohen, *Kibbutz Paths*, vol. 1 (Tel Aviv: Sifriat Poalim, 1973), p. 103. H.

20. A. Ruppin, *Dreissig Jahre Aufbau in Palestina* (Berlin: Schocken Verlag, 1937), p. 162.

21. Buber, *Paths in Utopia*, pp. 142-43.

2   Education in the Kibbutz

At every stage in the rearing of children in the kibbutz, from earliest infancy onward, there is a structured division in educational duties. Responsibility for the care of the growing child is divided between the family and the community, the latter in the form of caregivers and teachers. Such a dual-centered upbringing is not an uncommon one[1] and is, in fact, found in both Western and communist countries. In all cases, the family is regarded as an educational element which needs to be complemented from outside the parental home even from the child's earliest years. Yet the considerations which led to a division of duties vary from one system to another. The kibbutz does not face the problem of an underprivileged class in its midst which necessitates a solution to a socio-economic problem; nor does it contain among its members many parents who are unable to fulfill their parental role. Kibbutz education is not run by a state which imposes its regulations. The problem of parents who find it hard to adapt themselves to the new educational system does occur; but in the framework of the kibbutz, where all action is voluntary, it cannot be solved by relegating the parents to a subordinate role. Nor is the kibbutz a group which, for the sake of its political aims, has adopted an educational enterprise.

Let us see now what forces brought about a division of duties in child rearing in the kibbutz movement.

The first step toward communal education was taken in Degania while some of the bachelors in the small group were still not prepared to share responsibility for the upbringing of the children. When the first two children were born, the question of how they should be raised was left to the mothers to decide. It was no easy decision. The young mothers not only had to cope with all the problems and anxieties involved in raising infants far from the social and medical facilities of the town but also had to resolve an immediate, inner conflict. They were torn between their desire to devote all their time to the care of their child and the wish to participate fully in the work and social life of the group. The two mothers finally agreed to take turns in attending to both children. But one of them could not endure the separation from her son for any length of time. The kind of compromise she sought was one of the factors which led her to leave Degania and to participate in the establishment of a new form of settlement, the moshav, where the family is both the basic economic unit and the main agent in bringing up the children. The rest of the kibbutz members endorsed the principle formulated in 1916 by Joseph Bussel, their main spokesman on ideological matters. They agreed that financial responsibility for the children had to be shared by all the members, parents and single members alike, and that the children should be raised collectively. In 1919 communal education became the accepted system in Degania, with Chayuta Bussel serving as the first caregiver.

Although by 1924 it had become clear that the new system had been adopted by the kibbutzim, certain doubts as to its validity and value were still entertained, especially among the women. At a large gathering of all the existing kibbutzim held that year, many women argued that parents had no right to impose their ideals on the form of their children's upbringing and, in this way, to sacrifice the children to the needs of the community. "Life in the kvutza shatters the life of women," one of them contended bitterly. "They have achieved neither full participation in the life of the community nor a full family life." Their argument was countered by Joseph Bussel who regarded parental resistance to communal education as an illustration of the parental tendency to view the child as a personal possession and as an expression of parental desire to dominate the child, an expression which, in his opinion, was not conducive to community life. At the same gathering, Tabenkin, the spokesman of Kibbutz Meuchad, reminded his audience that many young people now live together without bringing children into the world and that some kibbutzim had even asked their members to abstain from marriage for the next five years to prevent an increase in the child population. Tabenkin emphasized that without children the kibbutz could never become a permanent way of life. But, in fact, while discussion on all aspects of the kibbutz child population was raging, communal education had already become an established system in all the existing kibbutzim.

What were the factors which brought about communal education? Were the members of the kibbutzim in some way influenced from outside? Y. Ron-Polani gives a reply to these questions. In all the printed and written sources available to him and in all his conversations with people involved in education, Ron-Polani tells us that he found no trace of external influence, neither by living example nor in a book which describes some kind of educational utopia or some applicable theory of communal education. He claims that the beginnings of communal education in the kibbutz were made in an attempt to ease the great strain imposed upon kibbutz members by hard living conditions, conditions so difficult as to make the rearing of children by a mother impossible unless she had the support and help of the group. The second factor which Polani mentions is the determination of a group of courageous women not to renounce their active part in the initiation of a new way of life for the sake of motherhood, for, as Chayuta Bussel put it, "Communal education is the first step towards woman's liberation."

Although Ron-Polani is correct in his claim that the initiation of communal education in Degania was a response to the pressing conditions of the time, there is no doubt that its continuation was greatly influenced by the pedagogic and psychological theories of the post-World War I period which the members of the third immigration wave, the Third Aliyah, brought with them, influenced by the revolutions in Europe and by changes in European contemporary thought.

The new type of education had to face an early test in the upbringing of a number of problem children, all in early adolescnece, who became the basis for the children's community established at Beth Alpha.[2] It lasted for four years only, from 1925 to 1929, beginning with 35 children and at no stage comprising more than 50. Few of the children were kibbutz-born; most were the children of relatives from Europe, either orphans or the product of broken homes. The educators in charge of this group had only the experience of their work as youth leaders in the HaShomer Hatzair movement in Europe. They had, however, read Freud and G. Wyneken,[3] and some had benefited from the opportunity in Vienna of observing S. Bernfeld's attempt to put modern educational theory into practice in his *Kinderheim Baumgarten*.[4] Thus equipped, the group of educators, led by E. Rapaport, a Viennese disciple of Buber, put into practice the new pedagogic principles which were then sweeping Europe. Rapaport summarizes them thus:

From formal education to knowledge acquired from life,
From the book to the physical work.
From a discipline based on blind obedience to a regime of activity and creation in an atmosphere of freedom.[5]

Ever since, kibbutz education has been deeply influenced by contemporary thought in psychology and education. There is evidence in the writings of early kibbutz educationalists that even from the early days they regarded kibbutz education not only as a means of making the lives of mother and child easier and more productive but also as an educational system in its own right. Looking back, S. Golan states, "Not hardship or economic necessity have moulded communal education; the form and content of communal education crystallized under the aegis of educational ideals and the image of a community longed for."[6]

There are today about 35,000 children growing up in a kibbutz environment and receiving kibbutz education.[a] A brief explanation of the social structure and the pedagogic content of kibbutz upbringing follows.

(1) Kibbutz education creates two centers in the life of the child—the parents' home and the children's house. Both have a deep impact on the child's life. Close cooperation between the two is of vital importance to the well-being of the child. If such cooperation functions as it should, the psychological advantage to the child is considerable. In various periods of kibbutz education, the importance attributed to parents in contrast to that of *metaplot* (caregivers) and

---

[a]In addition, 2000 children from town are being educated in the kibbutz.

teachers has varied. But at no time has there been an all-out attempt to exclude parental influence (as has been made in certain communes[7]). Parents themselves elect the committee which is invested with the educational authority of the kibbutz.

(2) At all ages, a group of peers is considered an important factor in the socializing processes of the child. Children grow up in peer groups from infancy onward.

(3) The kibbutz understands that only the existence of children can perpetuate the new social experiment and only a willingness to invest time, thought, and finance in education can prevent a small and rather homogeneous community from becoming an isolated and narrow-minded village. Thus, even when great hardship was the lot of all the adults, the children enjoyed superior conditions. In every newly established kibbutz, the children's house was a concrete building while the adults, more often than not, lived in tents or in wooden barracks. The children were always educated in small groups with a high ratio of educators—at the infant stage, 4 to 6 children in a group; at the nursery and primary school stage, 18 to 20 children in a class; and at secondary school level, about 25 children in a group. Child care reached such a high level that the infant mortality rate was not only strikingly low, considering the conditions of the Middle East, but even low by European middle-class standards. All kibbutz children receive education to the age of 18.

(4) Kibbutz education is antiauthoritarian. Modern educational trends with their criticism of class-conditioned authority in the family have made a major contribution to this approach. At the same time, the social framework of the kibbutz does not allow for any coercive authority in the child's upbringing,[8] since there is no economic dependence on permanent officials endowed with authority. As a result, the decision of a kibbutz-born youngster to become a member of the community in which he was raised cannot be imposed upon him. Such a decision usually stems from a feeling of identification with the values embodied in kibbutz living and from the feeling of being at home in the human and physical landscape of the kibbutz.

(5) The children's house plays an important role, especially at the infant stage, in the continuous process of identification with the values of the kibbutz world. Everything possible is done to make the children's house the children's home, so that it is far from being an institution in the normally accepted sense of the word. The house is furnished and equipped according to the needs of every age group: it is surrounded by a courtyard, well equipped for the growing child's needs, with flowers and bushes, hiding places, and playgrounds.[9]

(6) Under Freud's influence, the decisive contribution of the early years to personality development was recognized early in the kibbutz movement, and much thought has been devoted since to early child care. The emphasis has been on the fostering in the child of a sense of individuality, of creativity, and a basic trust as opposed to the detailed determination of developmental achievements to

be reached by every child at a fixed age, with one-sided emphasis on motor and language development.

(7) Two different forms of nursery schools are conducted in kibbutzim. One comprises children of the same age; the other prefers mixed age groups as a matter of pedagogic principle. Children from 3 to 7 years old are brought up in one group. The age of 7 is generally accepted as the proper age for school entrance.

(8) The administration of the kibbutz school in all three federations was originally governed by four main principles. First, schools were not considered only as institutes for teaching and learning. They were seen as a means of combining the whole range of youthful activities—study, social and cultural activities, work and play. The school was organized as a children's community, not as an institute of learning run only by the teachers.

The learning process is based on internal motivation with no recourse to marks and examinations. It was also decided that teaching methods should keep pace with the child's own speed and should be based on the child's personal interests. At all times, individuality should be encouraged. Last, it was believed the schools should work toward a value orientation in their students, especially at the age of adolescence. The emotional bond of the young child to his kibbutz provides a basis on which such an orientation can be built. From an emotional attachment to the kibbutz, the adolescent is led to an awareness of the values which govern kibbutz living and of its role in Israeli society, while at the same time he is brought to understand the problems inherent in both.

Needless to say, there have always been differences in the extent to which any given school has managed to realize its principles. These differences stem from many sources—the different characters of the teachers, pedagogic standards in any particular kibbutz, etc. While in primary schools the original principles are still adhered to in all three kibbutz federations, in secondary schools some of them have been questioned. This questioning has been brought about by recent changes in kibbutz life. Those demand the continuation of study at an academic level for the sake of satisfying both the demands of new tasks in industry, agriculture, and kibbutz management and the growing desire of kibbutz-born youngsters for self-realization through study. The demand for changes in the kibbutz schools has been voiced in particular by grown-up members of the second kibbutz generation. Their main argument is that previously the importance of study and specialization was underrated. This contention has been strongly voiced in all three kibbutz federations. Nevertheless, Kibbutz Artzi has stuck to the original concepts which governed children's communities for adolescents as well as for younger children, in the conviction that youth needs to live in its own realm and that this attitude in no way obstructs reform in teaching methods. The other two federations, however, have recently established joint district schools where adolescents study till midday and return afterward to their kibbutz. This change has created larger schools which find it easier to introduce specialization in studies. On the other hand, in the larger schools, the all-embracing character of the children's communities, with their emphasis on shared social activities, has of course diminished.[10]

(9) Education toward physical work is one of the main aims of all kibbutz federations and is considered a basic value fostered by the kibbutz. Such an attitude toward work clearly reflects the willing transition of Jewish town dwellers to a life close to nature and the esteem they gave to the adaptation to work in the basic areas of production. While at a young age the children work in their own little farm and provide their own services, at the adolescent stage work is done mainly in the kibbutz where the youngsters join with adults. The amazing capacity for and dexterity in physical work are one of the striking features of kibbutz youth.

(10) The kibbutz educator meets the child in many situations, and the child learns to regard him as the embodiment of kibbutz values. The rearing of the child in the kibbutz demands the provision of educators at every stage, including the preschool age groups. Since the type of education given is unique to the kibbutz, the duties of an educator cannot be satisfactorily carried out by a hired staff. In 1939, early recognizing the need for the educational training of kibbutz members, M Segal founded Seminar HaKibbutzim in Tel Aviv as a teacher training institute. Its northern branch, Oranim (founded in 1951), has gradually become the center for specific pedagogic activities in the kibbutz.

(11) Small groups and a high ratio of educators to children within the kibbutz educational system contribute to early recognition of behavioral disorders and neurotic problems in children. With a division of functions such as exists in the kibbutz, parents cannot conceal their child's problems. In a child-centered atmosphere, the desire to assist the problem child professionally has led to the establishment of three large child guidance clinics. In addition to the treatment which the child receives at the clinic, advice and help are given to parents, child, and all concerned with the child's education by special personnel, members of the kibbutz to which the child belongs, who have been trained at Oranim. Supporting therapy is thus rendered to those who need it in the child's home environment. M Kaffman, the director of the kibbutz clinics in Oranim and Tel Aviv, has summarized his twenty years of experience in clinical work with kibbutz children as follows.[11]

1. We have failed to uncover any clinical entity recognizable as a specific or prevalent emotional disturbance of kibbutz children. In fact, the usual psychiatric syndromes observed in children or adolescents raised in the traditional Western family may also be observed among kibbutz youngsters. It should be noted, however, that out of 3,000 emotionally-disturbed children referred to the kibbutz clinics, we have so far failed to reveal a single case of psychogenically determined early childhood psychosis.
2. On the other hand, the kibbutz system of upbringing permits the rearing of normal children showing an ample diversity of personality patterns, all of which are certainly covered by the wide concept of normalcy.

References

1. Yehuda Ron-Polani, *Until Here* (Tel Aviv: Am Oved, 1971). H. He has also published some of the relevant documents in "Letters on Education" of the Ichud, May 1973. H. Unless stated otherwise, all the quotations are from these publications.

2. Cf. Y. Ron-Polani, "The First Children's Community," *Until Here*. H.

3. Gustav Wyneken, *Schule and Jugendkultur* (Jena: Eugen Diederichs, 1913).

4. S. Bernfeld, *Kinderheim Baumgarten. Bericht Uber einen ernsthaften Versuch mit neuer Erziehung* (Berlin: Judischer Verlag, 1921).

5. Ron-Polani, *Until Here*.

6. S. Golan, "Upbringing in the Family, in Institutions and the Kibbutz," in *Sugiot* (Tel Aviv: Sifriat Poalim, 1956), p. 308. H.

7. In Oneida, for instance, cf. Rosabeth Moss Kanter, *Commitment and Community* (Cambridge, Mass.: Harvard University Press, 1972), pp. 12-14, 45, 91.

8. Cf. M. Gerson, "Authority in the Old Education and Authority in Socialist Education," in *Essays on Kibbutz Education* (Tel Aviv: Sifriat Poalim, 1968). H.

9. For detailed descriptive material on the children's house in early childhood, cf. Yona Ben-Yaakov, "Methods of Kibbutz Collective Education during Early Childhood," in *Growing Up in Groups*, ed. J. Marcus (New York: Gordon and Breach, 1972). Cf. also M. Segal, *The Children's House in the Change of Times* (Tel Aviv: Kibbutz Meuchad, 1975). H.

10. Y. Dar has investigated the problem of this new type of school in his booklet "Virtues and Deficiencies of My School," Ichud Research Institute, December, 1974 (mimeographed). H.

11. M. Kaffman, "Characteristics of the Emotional Pathology of the Kibbutz Child," *American Journal of Orthopsychiatry*, July 1972, p. 108. Cf. also Kaffman, "Family Conflict in the Psychopathology of the Kibbutz Child," in *Family Process*, 1972: 11, 171-188.

3 Women in the Kibbutz

The first condition for the liberation of the wife is to bring the whole female sex back into public industry and this in turn demands the abolition of the monogamous family as the economic unit of society.

Friedrich Engels, 1846.

Within the kibbutz setting, the demands of the modern woman for equal opportunities and status seem to have been satisfied. Women are free and even encouraged to undertake work outside the immediate confines of the home. The burden of household chores is greatly relieved by communal cooking, laundry, and mending facilities, and it is expected that the remaining duties will be shared by the spouses. Women are no longer dependent economically on men. Every woman works in the kibbutz economy; and since there are no wages, there can be no wage differentiation according to sex. There is no conflict between the roles of mother and worker; the kibbutz system allows a woman to fulfill both roles with no fear of unemployment during pregnancy or child neglect during the mother's working hours. In her attitude to work and social activities and to finding a solution to the practical problems involved in both, the mother is supported by the kibbutz. Official kibbutz philosophy demands that women play a part in all spheres of social activity while the kibbutz organization shares the upbringing and education of the children. In relations between the sexes, there are no double standards of sexual morality; birth control methods are available to all.

These are achievements of which any women's liberation organization would be proud. Yet, as we shall see later, institutional arrangements do not of themselves eliminate prejudices and create a new attitude to sex typing. We shall suggest that it is necessary to initiate further changes—educational and administrative—before the needs of an overwhelming majority of kibbutz women can be fully satisfied.

It is impossible to consider the needs of kibbutz women for self-expression and equal status in isolation. These aspirations are shared by women in many parts of the world, and many of their achievements are paralleled as a result of either institutional arrangements, as in Russia, or a struggle by the women themselves, as in the United States. Their main aim is to eliminate sex role typing. Let us now examine the mechanism of sex typing more closely and see how it affects the roles of both men and women.[1]

The unnatural generally means only uncustomary and . . . every thing which appears usual is natural. The subjection of women to men being a universal custom, any departure from it quite naturally appears unnatural. John Stuart Mill, 1869.

In modern times, three profound changes in the life pattern of woman have come about.[2] First, women are now in a position to regulate the number of children they want to have. Second, the life expectancy of women is now 75 years, thirty years beyond the child-bearing age. Last, technological developments have altered the nature of labor to such an extent that today most work requires more dexterity than physical strength. These changes which have revolutionized the life of the modern woman have also opened up new avenues of activity to her. Theoretically, the world is now all before her. Yet, in practice discrimination against women is still very much with us. We may well ask why this is so, and if there are unchangeable factors, of a biological or a psychological nature, which render the idea of sex equality nothing more than a pious wish. We shall deal with these theoretical questions in brief.[3] The purpose of our discussion is primarily to provide a background for the appraisal of kibbutz phenomena and problems, which we shall deal with later.

Paul Mussen[4] has affirmed that the fact of being born a boy does not make him automatically "masculine" in behavior and emotional responses. It is only through social sex typing that he acquires the sex role which, in his culture, is regarded as appropriate. Modern research has shown that there are differences between boys and girls which start at birth or appear during the first year of their development.[5] Of course, no form of socialization can reverse the rudiments of innate sex differences. But the process of socialization can and does reinforce them, deliberately widening what were initially small sex differences until differences in behavior between boys and girls become increasingly manifest. We expect to see, and we do see, greater physical activity and aggressiveness in boys and greater sensitivity to pain in girls. Similarly, boys receive more parental pressure to channel their aggressiveness into culturally recognized patterns, while girls are encouraged to conform by being rewarded for their goodness. The basis on which self-esteem for boys is built is that of achievement; for girls, that of winning affection. In the case of both boys and girls, socialization inhibits the expression of disapproved behavior, often by forcing its sublimation. It is made clear to the child that differential behavior in both sexes is "natural" and therefore desirable, worthy of both recognition and reward by society. Active women are thus often labeled as existentially deviant; they are regarded as poor souls who lack sex appeal and the personal fulfillment to be obtained in a happy family life. Even at a young age, the tomboy has a difficult life. Afraid of her isolation and her future personal unhappiness, her family and friends usually make great efforts to "heal" her from her nonfeminine inclinations. Her achievement orientation is often discouraged on the grounds that men prefer less gifted girls. Similarly, the little boy or adolescent youth who shows introspective tendencies and empathy toward his peers is prodded toward a different approach; he is encouraged to be extroverted and outgoing, characteristics which are portrayed as those most fitting a man. What is most harmful in this sort of training is the insistence that individual men and women are unable to cross sex lines in behavior effectively, an assumption which necessarily results in the waste of much individual talent. It takes great individual strength for a woman to achieve prominence in politics or for a man to become a "soft-hearted" lyrical poet.

Sex stereotyping is hard to eliminate; 160 years have passed since Jane Austen wrote her sad words of resignation to woman's lot: "Without thinking highly either of men or of matrimony, marriage had always been her object; it was the only honourable provision for well educated young women of small fortune, and however uncertain of giving happiness must be their pleasantest preservation from want."[6] Even though social conditions have greatly changed in modern times, the idea that motherhood and housekeeping are the "natural" role of women is still widely held. Simone de Beauvoir has rightly said that it is absurd to shroud the drudgery of the daily cleaning and washing with its endless repetition in a romantic cloud of words which speak of woman's destiny and fulfillment.[7]

Motherhood, the cardinal traditional role of woman, is a very different matter. It surely gives deep emotional satisfaction and many moments of absolute joy. But one should not ignore its less positive aspects. Motherhood as a full-time occupation is a new social role, restricted to a small circle of women even today. Since it deprives women of a clear social role, it seems that these women are often beset by doubts concerning their own importance and are often full of complaints of the long hours of isolation in suburbia. Alice Rossi[8] has described well the excessive dependence of children raised by such mothers and the widespread reaction against "Momism" it frequently evokes. On the other hand, the prejudice against women's work outside the home on the grounds that it results in a psychologically deprived child has a powerful emotional effect on women, arousing in them deep-seated feelings of guilt. But its factual basis is questionable, to say the least. It has been shown[9] that work outside the home, especially when the mother *enjoys* her employment, has a positive effect on both mother and child. The mother obtains a greater measure of security while the child develops a fuller understanding of social roles in modern society. He sees in his mother a living example of a way of life worthy of emulation in that it contributes to the well being of both the individual and society.[a]

In the third aspect of woman's traditional role, that of marriage partner, the most rigorous sex typing is found. In a traditional marriage relationship, the husband is considered the breadwinner; the wife, the household manager, often with disastrous consequences for both. Bettelheim has defined well the situation which frequently occurs when marriage is regarded as sufficient to ensure the

---

[a]This holds, of course, only under two conditions: that the child is well cared for and that the mother starts work only when the child has reached about its third year.

happiness of the woman. As a consequence, women often invest overheàvily in their husbands and children, yet are frequently frustrated because husbands and children do not have an equal need for emotional overinvestment.[10] Those women who invest their achievement efforts and self-esteem overwhelmingly in maternity do not realize that with increased longevity and smaller families motherhood is a role which disappears when children are independent, thus leaving a long period of their life void of content.[11] Traditional sex role distribution is usually discussed in relation to its effect on women. But there are other aspects as well. Gronseth,[12] a sociologist from Norway, stresses that the definition of the husband as *the* breadwinner is the foremost obstacle in the way of sex equality: it justifies lower salaries for women as well as the nonparticipation of the husband in domestic tasks (which would waste his highly paid time); men commit suicide much more frequently than women, are excessive alcohol misusers, and are punished for criminality almost 50 times as often as women.

Unfortunately, in trying to escape from rigid sex typing, some women's movements take the male model as the standard and renounce any difference between the sexes. This egalitarian approach reflects a deep, mostly unconscious dependence on man. In fact, equality between the sexes implies a change of the strictly differential definition of sex roles and greater freedom for both sexes to adopt roles which, according to present sex-typing rules, are deviant. Equality between the sexes implies that in such matters as intellect, politics, and occupation, men and women will be given equal opportunities for advancement. Because there is good reason to believe that some sex differences are present from an early age (as we have already indicated), even in a society based on true equality between the sexes, certain inherent differences may cause greater orientation toward practical achievement in men and toward interpersonal relations in women. If this is so, the community is obliged to ascribe the same social status and to give the same measure of practical assistance to both orientations. In the kibbutz, for instance, tasks carried out by women in child rearing and in other services should be treated as making a contribution to the success of the community equal to the contribution made by those who work in production. The creation of such an attitude to all kinds of work within the kibbutz demands much thought and inventive ability because within the kibbutz framework it cannot be attained simply by the granting of equal financial reward. Yet to reach this kind of equality would be a truly historic achievement, a victory over the position which Margaret Mead has described as the core of sex discrimination: every society known at present has assigned the things most worth doing to men; if men are making baskets, this is regarded as the most important activity.[13]

But it is not only in the field of work that equality can and should be achieved. Other avenues are also open. The achievement needs of liberated women can be directed not only to areas which are different from those usually preferred by men, but also to preeminent political positions where they might devise their own particular style of expression. It is to be expected that in different periods of a woman's life different orientations will prevail, depending on her physical condition and needs. At one period in her life, the emphasis may be on achievement, at another on interpersonal relations. The ridicule heaped upon the active woman is nothing but an attempt to divert attention from the real issue, which for both men and women lies in the need to allow real choice in all spheres of activity, choice made according to individual talent and inclination and not according to rigid differential sex typing that impoverishes both the individual and society.

A recent book by L. Tiger and J. Shepher[14] has made an interesting contribution to the discussion on the origin of sex differences.[15] The authors regard the development of women's position in the kibbutz as decisive proof of the predominance of biological factors in sex differences. Put in a nutshell, their argument runs as follows. In the kibbutz, ideal conditions for full sexual equality have been created. The socialization of children is equalitarian; there is no early sex typing (p. 165); sex differentiation is slow until the beginning of reproductive life (p. 181). Yet even under these conditions, women are not content with their lot because they do not have enough familism (p. 259). This state of affairs proves that most men and women will not be very responsive to social changes that could blur the sexual polarization (p. 240). In accordance with the dictates of a biogrammar, women seek association with their offspring, an association which is specieswide, but which is not provided for in the kibbutz (p. 272). This violation of the biogrammar cannot last long and cannot be carried out by many people without causing serious problems for both the individual and society (pp. 265 and 274).

A critical examination of this updated version of the age-old belief that there are unchangeable, natural sex differences, which operate in the kibbutz as well, will involve us in a brief examination of the attitudes of the founders of the kibbutz to the role of women.

Today women form 48.3 percent of the total adult kibbutz population.[b] In a way of life intended to foster the potential of all kibbutz members, many women of the founder generation are now expressing their disappointment.[16] Middle-aged women who used to find much satisfaction in the field of early child education often have difficulty in cooperating with younger, second-generation women whose manner of working with young children is less principled and more easygoing. Older women frequently find that their kibbutz career has not provided them with a skill; so in their middle years they are restricted in the type of work which is open to them. As a result, some feel that their interests and the fulfillment of their psychological needs may become too exclusively focused on their children and grandchildren; and from their own

---

[b]The distribution of women is not equal in all kibbutzim; in young kibbutzim, the proportion of women is lower.

experience in middle-class homes, they know the psychological risks entailed in such a restriction. Some of them are surprised by the reemergence of feelings of which they thought they had ridded themselves when they joined the kibbutz (or even earlier, in the youth movement), namely, feelings of female inferiority and dependence on male esteem. One cannot make these feelings evaporate by labeling them as mere caprices, typical of middle or old age. They are based on facts, as we shall soon see.

How Did It Happen?

In order to understand the present situation, it will be helpful to return to the earliest period of the kibbutzim. We have already mentioned that the decision to join a kibbutz was a difficult one to make for all members, but particularly so for women. After being raised in the traditional, sheltered atmosphere of middle-class Jewish homes, women found it hard to face the hardships of the new life, not least among them to fight against male prejudice in order to win the right to work and to be accepted as an equal member in the group. The Jewish colonizing institutions employed men only. The women who became an economic burden were not really considered as meriting equal status in the group. Even in the first kvutza, when the group started to build its life autonomously, the approach to women's work did not change fundamentally.

Ron-Polani quotes the recollections of some women from this early period:[17]

There were men in our group who regarded our wish to work in the fields as a breach of the so-called natural order; who neither believed in our physical and spiritual ability nor our wish to do so; who were not interested in our participation in group debates which deal with general questions of the labor movement.

Or

The men are not interested in our participation at talks about general problems which concern every worker.

And at a later period:

In the Diaspora we had been members of Hechalutz with equal rights. But immediately when we arrived in Palestine a division was made between two groups: Those who build the country and those who have to care for the builders.

Thus it is obvious that sex discrimination has existed from the very beginnings of the kibbutzim. In the harsh conditions of the early years, physical strength and endurance were required to tackle agricultural work, attributes which only a few women could muster. Later when technology made certain agricultural and technical tasks easier, a redivision of assignment was not considered a matter of principle, because attitudes toward sex differentiation in work duties had already become deeply entrenched.

Nor was rigid sex differentiation confined to the area of work. Lilia Basse-wich, who immigrated in the early 1920s to Palestine, has vividly described the struggle women had to lead in Ein Harod for their right to participate actively in the organization for self-defense.[18] Their struggle was intensified after the bitter experience of the women being "protected," locked in a cowshed in Ein Harod during the Arab riots of 1929. Bassewich states explicitly in her paper that the struggle of the women for participation in defense activities was felt to be not only a struggle for the fulfillment of a national need but also part of the struggle against male domination. Bassewich also initiated in Kibbutz Meuchad an at-tempt to secure the active participation of women in committee work and in representation, both on the local level and in the kibbutz federation as a whole, using organizational means. Because of the support given by leaders such as Tabenkin, her propsal—that at least one-third of the members serving on any committee be women—was adopted. In theory, this organizational measure still applies. In practice, however, it is not so often implemented. Ten years later, in Kibbutz Artzi, a proposal was made by Yona Golan (supported by some male leaders, though not by the political leadership) to organize a special section for women where they would deal with both general and specific questions without male leadership. This proposal has never been accepted. It was branded a diver-sion from the sacred principle of women's equality because it was felt that women should be chosen to serve the community in their own right, as indi-viduals, and not as representatives of their sex.

Objections to Golan's scheme came in the main from a certain type of women belonging to the founder generation who regarded political activity as the most important expression of social involvement for both men and women. The same type of personality also scornfully rejected any interest in beauty culture as betraying an adherence to middle-class values. For them, a lack of interest in personal appearance went together with a burning sense of urgency and mission and with absolute belief in an equalitarian approach to all problems.

The early years of the kibbutzim were a period of great hardship and great enthusiasm. The elation of starting from scratch and the sense of being granted a unique opportunity to found a new communal way of life pervaded every aspect of an existence that was reduced to bare essentials, physical work by day and guard duty at night. For women in this very demanding and highly charged atmosphere, an egalitarian attitude held many attractions, especially in the sphere of work. Participation in agricultural work became for them the major proof of their belonging to the budding community. While it was accepted that some women had to take on traditional female duties in the kitchen and the nursery, women occupied in this way were not made to feel that they shared in the glory of work concerned with the redemption of the land; nor did they experience the same sense of revolutionary change enjoyed by the members occupied in other, more "productive" tasks. For both economic and ideological reasons, the specifically feminine tasks were not classified as productive work in the files of the work organizers. Although many of the women working in the service branches and in education contributed far more than a mere "productive" day of work by laying the foundations for a new system of communal education and by their work in a communal kitchen which catered to all the needs of each individual member, they rarely met the appreciation and encouragement reserved for women who worked in agriculture. In contrast to their cardinal thesis, Tiger and Shepher have illustrated the existence of sex discrimination in the spheres of work inside the four kibbutzim they studied. They show that from the earliest days of these kibbutzim, only 11 percent of the women ever worked in branches that were regarded as men's work while an even smaller percentage of men worked in branches considered more suited to women. What is most significant is that those men worked there on a temporary, not a permanent basis.[19] Tiger and Shepher also claim that only lip service was paid to the principle of sexual equality in the participation of women in political matters.

The approach of Kibbutz Artzi and of its youth movement, HaShomer Hatzair, was based on the assumption that the problem of women derived from their social status.[20] In order to bring about full equality, it was agreed that women should be allowed to enter all spheres of work open to men and to carry out any social duties assigned to men. These early tenets of the movement make it clear that the original concept of sex equality among members of the founder generation was an egalitarian one; i.e., male qualities and activities were set forth as the model for both sexes. This attitude stigmatized vital spheres of work, such as the children's house and the kitchen, as unproductive. It is likely that this approach left kibbutz women with a distrust of slogans calling for their liberation and planted the seeds for their disillusionment. This seems to be the source of many of the ambivalent feelings and perplexities which are confusing the issues concerning the position of women in the kibbutz. In the 1950s, three main factors brought about increased sex differentiation in the kibbutz. First, an increase in the size of families resulted in a growing need for caregivers in the children's houses. Second, a rise in the standard of living increased the number of personnel needed for service duties. Third, the increasing scale and mechanization of agriculture created demands for greater technical skill and spatial mobility. These changes made it even more difficult for women to continue in agricultural work.

Tiger and Shepher have shown[21] that the sexual division of labor has at present reached 70 to 80 percent and that this polarization is greater among people socialized in the kibbutz than among those socialized outside it. As far as committee work is concerned,[c] Tiger and Shepher have shown that among committee chairmen the proportion of men is much higher and that they pre-

---

[c]Activity in committees is voluntary and is carried out after working hours.

dominate in the membership of central committees, with a high level of authority (p. 142). In the face of these facts, one can hardly rid oneself from the suspicion that an age-old ideology is recurring here, namely that social esteem should be given to the breadwinner, to the man who earns the money.

A situation riddled with contradictions has thus developed in this area of kibbutz life. These contradictions emerged clearly as early as 1955 in a large-scale research undertaken by the author.[22] It was based on a questionnaire which was answered individually by 638 girls from Kibbutz Artzi and Kibbutz Meuchad, equal representatives of age groups between 13 and 18 years.[d] The research disclosed a systematic difference in approach between the two federations and, less clearcut, between the younger and the older age groups investigated. Preference for agricultural work was expressed by 87 percent of the respondents in Kibbutz Artzi (KA) as opposed to 49 percent in Kibbutz Meuchad (KM). The main reason given in the replies for a preference for outdoor work was "attractiveness of productive work" while "physical difficulty" and "effect on feminine beauty" were given as the justification for a negative attitude to agricultural work. A quotation from the statement of a 16-year-old girl from Kibbutz Artzi enables us to glance into the psychological dynamics which brought about the positive approach:

Work in the children's house is degrading, but if a very young girl [fourteen] is sent there instead of working in the fields, it may appeal to her from various points of view. Work in the children's house is easier. But it is necessary to overcome this attraction and to work in the fields. Apart from this, there is something shameful in loving work in the children's house and we struggle with all our might against working there. I do not like to work there.

Small wonder that when asked if they would like to work in the children's house, 84 percent of the respondents in KA replied in the negative as against 47 percent in KM. In both federations, as the age of the respondents increased, the approach to work in the children's house became gradually more positive. But in KM the declared approach to agricultural work became more negative as the girls grew, while in KA it remained positive in all the age groups. The last question asked was whether the respondents considered that in the kibbutz women have achieved full equality with men. In both movements, the answers became increasingly negative as the respondents increased in age, but the overall difference between the proportion of negative responses given by members of the two federations was very marked: the question was answered in the negative by 44 percent in KM and by 85 percent in KA.

How can we interpret such results? It seems likely that as the girls grow and become increasingly familiar with and aware of the realities of life in the kib-

---

[d]We shall deal here only with the first part of the research, which concerned the approach to work.

butz, they are influenced by these realities far more strongly than by ideological teachings. This, however, does not apply to the cult of agricultural work in Kibbutz Artzi, which by then was deeply and "orthodoxically" entrenched in its educational system. Thus, in Kibbutz Artzi a response was produced which was in contradiction to social facts, with all the adverse educational results such a situation entails. In contrast, Kibbutz Meuchad was far more empirical in its educational value system; by the 1950s there were few women still engaged in work in agricultural branches.[e]

Twenty years have passed since this study was carried out. During this period, differences in the attitudes of men and women to their work and social activities have grown considerably. For many women, family life has become the prime consideration, while work and social activities have taken second place; men usually reverse this order of priorities. Yet it should be noted that in Kibbutz Artzi only 37 percent of the women respondents said that they felt this order to be desirable.[23] The other 63 percent probably experience the pangs of cognitive dissonance. Their inner conflict is likely to be much stronger than that Alice Rossi has described[24] in a situation where women's work outside the home is optional, while in the kibbutz every woman is expected to work in the community.

If one adheres to an explanation of sexual differences which regards social facts as those which predominantly influence attitudes, one would expect the traditional sex role division to be stronger among women of the second kibbutz generation. Where their mothers rebelled against a social system and within it against traditional sex roles and struggled with inner conflicts and disappointments, the younger generation has been raised under conditions in which a differential order of sex roles prevails. Many of them accept these conditions as unchangeable. If they do, we should not be surprised by any possible desire on their part to glorify their task by acceptance of the "women's natural role" ideology.

And, indeed, in Rosner's survey it was found that second-generation women included in his sample had fewer qualms about women's place in the kibbutz than their mothers' generation had. The reasons are not hard to find. In the past fifteen years, conditions of work and of life in the kibbutz have been greatly ameliorated for the mother. After childbirth, she enjoys a lenient schedule of work, and during her children's infancy her work schedule is geared to enable her to spend more time with them than was possible for parents of the founder generation. The home is no longer a tent or one-room apartment but a 2½-room apartment, equipped with modern appliances to ease the burden of housework.

---

[e]It is evident here that adolescent girls are even ready to accept conceptions of their sex role which are in contrast to their surrounding reality. This is an indication that the process of sex typing is not only more complex but also more modifiable than the adherents of "women's natural role" assume.

A widespread acceptance of the traditional role of women by the second generation is indicated by the fact that girls in the kibbutz now marry young, many of them at the age of 20 when they complete their military service. Although it is easier for women in the kibbutz to acquire professional training, the opportunity for training and job involvement which kibbutz life offers is quite frequently rejected by them. Many of them also prefer an early ritual confirmation of their sexual partnership, even though kibbutz morality allows for young couples to live together without legal sanction.

Changing the Status Quo

Yet there are also many exceptions to this generalization. Many young women share fully the achievement-oriented outlook which characterizes the second-generation male members of the kibbutz. These are the women for whom the desire to change results from their observations of the present condition of women in the kibbutz. One of them told me her disillusionment pointedly: "It is well known that women in the kibbutz play second fiddle." Their chance to exert an active influence on developments in the kibbutz would be enhanced if there were a separate organizational framework which would enable women to discuss their position and their problems on their own.

There are two ways of coping with this disillusionment. The first is simply to accept the preference for family life over work and over community life and to support familistic tendencies. The other is to forge the disappointment into a lever for change. We believe the second solution to be the one most consistent with kibbutz principles. In our eyes, a failure to fully utilize the potential of women members poses a threat to the future of kibbutz life. In itself, the maintenance of the kibbutz as a comparatively small socialist cell in a capitalist society is fraught with risk. If, in addition, half its population find life in the kibbutz frustrating and seek to effect a radical change by introducing a mere family-oriented way of life, there is a real threat to its survival.

The great achievements in the position of women that the kibbutz has to its credit are mainly in the sphere of institutional change. Yet they have not secured full equality of the sexes. It is this ostensible contradiction which has led Tiger and Shepher to their fundamental conclusions: Kibbutz living violates the bio-grammar and familistic tendencies which are a "natural" way of restoring a "natural" situation. As we have seen, there are in fact many factors of *social* character in kibbutz life which have prejudiced attempts to change the condition of women in the kibbutz. Tiger and Shepher themselves regard in general the argument of a "male conspiracy" against women as a weighty one. They define it as a powerful influence which induces women to accept an inferior status and also to adjust their offspring to it (p. 266). In their opinion, this does not apply to the kibbutz because the kibbutz "established itself in the aggressive search for sexual equity." Yet we have seen that in fact, because of an erroneous egalitarian conception, women in the kibbutz have been discriminated against from the beginning. Another basic error is their assertion that the natural attraction between mother and child is not allowed for in the kibbutz (p. 272). The writers err also in contending that women are only "somewhat more limited" than men in the choice of jobs (p. 181) and that sex typing becomes clear only at adolescence (p. 166). In fact, women have always been discriminated against: conditions in the service branches are often much worse than in production; women were granted fewer opportunities for further education than men; sex typing starts at the tender age, i.e. in the most formative years. In other words, we do not yet have a society in which perfect equality is being offered to women, an equality which the women reject, as Tiger and Shepher contend.[f]

Since the authors assume that equal status and equal opportunities have always been granted to women and they contrast the social reality with this ideal situation, it is easy to see how they come to their conclusion. It does seem that women are turning their backs on the openings proffered to them and are retreating into the "natural" world of the family. In fact, however, this ideal situation does not, as yet, exist. Familistic tendencies, we argue, are a reaction to a system in which there is covert, if not overt, discrimination. Remove the latter and you will be on the way to eliminating the former. In our opinion, Tiger and Shepher's book does little but give support to those in favor of familistic tendencies.

The most important question of the moment is whether there is a chance of overcoming the profound disillusionment which has beset many women in the kibbutz, whether there is a way of changing the situation. But before we deal with the problem of change, perhaps we should mention an additional factor that has complicated attempts to change the status of women in the kibbutz. The founder generation, including even those members who objected to Marxism, shared its overoptimistic belief that a radical change of social institutions and conditions automatically and quickly brings about a corresponding change in psychological makeup. But, in fact, change in attitude is a complex and prolonged process. In the light of our generation's experience of developments in Soviet Russia, we should have known that radical changes in human attitudes cannot be imposed institutionally and do not occur so quickly in society. Similarly, we should have learned from the lengthy and intricate process of change in belief systems which accompanied the transition from feudalism to capitalism, Max Weber recorded. But the fact is that we did not think along these lines. Our enthusiasm for the chance of building a new society from scratch prevented us from seeing such realities. The ensuing lack of insight had two unfortunate consequences. It was felt that change would come about in due course by itself

---

[f]It should be noted that their inquiry (apart from using census figures) was carried out in four kibbutzim only, hardly a representative sample.

and, therefore, there was no need to aid its development by conscious effort and organizational means. At the same time, the overoptimism of that period apparently had an adverse influence on women in the kibbutz. In the eagerness of their struggle toward the radical egalitarianism of the early days, they were willing to discard their traditional role but were disappointed to find that the fulfillment they expected did not materialize. It is, therefore, easy to understand their deep disillusionment.

Every woman had to try to build her new sex role in isolation, without the support of other women who shared her problems, without the support of institutional measures such as proportional representation of women in committees, and without adequate opportunity to learn a new sex role. Her attempts were hampered by sex segregation in work and, to a lesser degree, in committees. In the early days of the kibbutz, in every field of endeavor, new roles had to be learned and acquired in practice; the present-day managers of kibbutz economy certainly did not bring their skills with them when they joined the kibbutz fresh from the youth movement. Yet women in the kibbutz were hardly ever given the chance of fostering economic or managerial talent through practice in branches other than those connected with nutrition or interpersonal relations. Progressive optimists may believe that, given the chance, women will immediately show the same efficiency as men in every area of activity. For the sake of realism, however, one should acknowledge that today men have a greater chance of being self-confident, outgoing, and enterprising. This is a result of historical conditions, conditions which have prevailed for centuries and whose importance should not be overlooked. The kind of rash optimism which disregards these facts in the end will only strengthen male discrimination against women, which may then present itself as verified by experience. In fact, there is a need for effort, made patiently and consciously over a long time, by representatives of both sexes in order to overcome the results of discrimination against women. This effort has to take into account that in both sexes differences in talent and inclination exist and that, therefore, both men and women should be encouraged to participate actively in economic and managerial tasks. They should be given a chance to learn gradually and through practice the outgoing attitude and self-confidence which are needed to cope with these activities and which have come to be regarded as typically male characteristics. If this chance is not offered to women, the present state of strict sex differentiation in the kibbutz will perpetuate itself.

It is encouraging that there seems to be at least one country—Sweden—which is succeeding in bringing about changes in traditional sex roles. In an admirable paper,[25] Olof Palme has clearly defined the call for the abolition of rigid sex typing. The suppression of ability in women is one ill effect of sex discrimination. One of the greatest disadvantages of sex typing is the reduced share that men have in the upbringing of their children with the resulting negative effect on the child, especially on boys. As long as the duties of the male in society are recognized a priori as unalterable and the sole responsibility for household and children continues to be regarded as belonging "naturally" to the woman, talking about women's economic equality is meaningless. Legislation should effectively refute the view that economic security for women can be guaranteed only through marriage. Such legislation would thereby encourage the professional ambitions of women. In socialist Sweden, government authority, so often misused in human history, is directed toward the establishment of this approach. Individual taxation, instead of the traditional family taxation, has been introduced. Thus the partner working at home (the *hemmaman*, i.e., house-husband) has a legally recognized position. Another far-reaching reform has been introduced in education, its purpose being to counteract early sex typing. Schools make it clear to pupils that differences between individuals of the same sex are greater than average differences between the sexes as a whole.

We do not know how the recent change of government in Sweden will modify these processes. In any case, it would be hasty to assume that a reform of this magnitude could fully achieve its aims in a short time. Sweden does not offer a perfect solution to the problems of every individual and family unit, as the high suicide rate and reports of widespread problems in family life testify. The official sources of information published under Palme's premiership described frankly the difficulties experienced and the resistance to the new measures that is especially entrenched in the older generation and in capitalist circles. They mention the difficulties women have to face on the labor market, as a result of earlier inferior educational opportunities. Even with the help of a state apparatus, these radical changes apparently cannot be achieved in one generation. One result, at least, is already apparent. The supporters of the status quo can no longer invest themselves with an aura of sanctity, claiming that only theirs is a scientific approach or plain commonsense approach when they declare that any attempted change of traditional sex roles is impractical because it contradicts human nature.

If we compare the chances for reform in sex roles in the kibbutz to the chances for such change which exist in Sweden, two differences immediately become apparent. First, the kibbutz has no power of legislation. It cannot even assume that legislation in Israel will necessarily be sympathetic toward the kibbutz and toward changes of this kind. Second, many of the factors which motivated change in Sweden are absent in the kibbutz. In the kibbutz, both parents are able to play an active role in the raising of their children and to work in the kibbutz economy. In the kibbutz, since there is no economic competition, the price for success is less exacting; in the kibbutz, trial marriage has long been available to couples who wish it. It sounds paradoxical, but I believe that these achievements do not serve as a driving force toward the next stage of emancipation for the woman. They may even be an obstacle. Change in the kibbutz cannot be imposed from above but only through persuasion and by the attainment of consensus of opinion. Frequently I have been asked by well-meaning American friends why men are not drafted into work in the children's houses and women drafted into central managerial positions. The experience with political coercion that we have undergone in our lifetime can hardly encourage any socialist to rely on coercive measures. Such action would certainly be contrary to the voluntary structure of kibbutz life. The only way to bring about a change in sex roles in the kibbutz is the hard way, namely, by gradually altering the climate of personal relations and of public opinion. And to do this, one has to convince both men and women of the necessity for change. First-generation women, disillusioned by previous failures in attempts to implement changes, have to be convinced that change is possible, that a new phase in the old debate does not mean merely another declaration of elevated ideas, but real changes. The young women have to be convinced that the existing state of affairs is not the best possible, that the sex role problem is not only an individual but also a general problem in society. It should be dealt with in small groups of women concerned with "consciousness raising." Raising the consciousness of women and their self-liberation from sex role stereotypes is a precondition for their true emancipation.[26] It is only through cultivation of group solidarity among women that they will be able to play their full part in kibbutz activities. Until now, all too frequently, active women had to face grudging criticism by other women who regarded them as strange outsiders lacking in social adaptability.

In order to convince men that a change in attitude is both desirable and possible, it may be necessary to concentrate on other foci. The first step may need to be the development of a growing awareness among men that the present division of sex roles not only impoverishes the wife, with its related effect on family life, but also endangers the future of the kibbutz as a whole. Men holding managerial positions will have to admit to themselves that in a voluntary community, economic efficiency can never be separated from social considerations. The psychology which declares "My time is too precious to waste in housework" is not good enough as a guide to the distribution of duties in the kibbutz. Of course, a viable change cannot ignore the fact that a socialist cell inside a capitalist economy must be concerned with the need for profitability. But its planning has to include social considerations as well, and these must take into account a woman's inclinations toward any particular branch of production as well as the importance of joint work and social activities between the sexes, where each contributes according to talent and inclination. The atmosphere created by such changes will most certainly increase the number of families in which housework is shared by husband and wife. Equality between the sexes in domestic duties is of great significance, both as a practical way of coping with a chore and as a manifestation of fundamental attitude. Imposing domestic duties on women alone will necessarily increase any inclination they may have to give preference to household duties over work in one of the branches of the kibbutz.

In the sphere of work, the aim is not, of course, a radical abolition of sex differentiation. Even today, when many branches of work demand less physical effort, physical strength is still a factor to be considered. Therefore, the aim here should be to offer a variety of occupations which will provide greater choice for women, to demand professionalism in child care and in the services, to ensure a more equal distribution of boring work between men and women, and to firmly demand the abolition of obsolete sex prejudices. There is no reason, biological or social, why a woman cannot be an electrician or a technical drafter, why a woman cannot be a chief accountant rather than an assistant, or why women teachers cannot staff 50 percent of the high school positions, instead of being limited mainly to primary schools where they hold approximately 90 percent of the positions. The process of diversification of women's work can be eased if they are encouraged to enter additional fields set up recently in the work schedule of the kibbutz, such a social worker, efficiency expert, etc.

Educators in the kibbutz will have to revise their thinking in order to find ways to overcome the traditional sex typing which has developed in the wake of increasing sex role differentiation and which manifests itself in "sex-adapted" choice of toys, clothes, and behavior; for while this kind of sex-typing may enhance the probability of succeeding in traditional sex roles, in a community whose aim is equality between the sexes, any education toward the old image of the pleasing and submissive female will efficiently counteract any change in sex roles which is aspired to. Independence and achievement have to be fostered in the socialization of both sexes. Otherwise, adolescent girls in the kibbutz will soon learn to regard interpersonal relations as their only route to identity, leaving to boys the primacy of achievement in physical and intellectual work. So far, little empirical material on the process of socialization of the sexes in the kibbutz is available. But there are some phenomena in adolescence[g] which seem to warrant our apprehension.

A voluntary community cannot long tolerate incongruity between its aims and the process of socialization. What is needed now is a new concept of woman, one which takes for granted the value of marriage and motherhood but also acknowledges woman's need for creativity, independence, and achievement. The change in concept which we put forward here is necessary for the kibbutz if both waste of individual talent and perpetuation of inner conflict in its women are to be prevented and the growth of familistic tendencies halted.

References

1. Judity Hole and Ellen Levine, *Rebirth of Feminism* (New York: Quadrangle Books, 1971), p. 441.

2. Cf. M. Pollack, "Changing the Role of Women," *American Journal of Orthopsychiatry*, no. 5, special section on the women's movement; also Louisa Kapp Howe, ed. *The Future of the Family* (New York: Simon & Schuster,

[g]Cf. Chapter 5, part 3.

1972), pp. 56, 202–205, henceforth referred to as *Future*. Marlene Dixon, "The Rise of Women's Liberation," in J.M. Bardwick, *Readings on the Psychology of Women* (New York: Harper and Row, 1972).

3. J.M. Tanner and Barbel Inhelder, eds., *The Childhood Genesis of Sex Differences in Behavior*, vol. 3 of *Discussions on Child Development* (London: Tavistock Publications, 1963). Ed. E. Maccoby and C.N. Jacklin, *The Psychology of Sex Differences* (Stanford, Conn.: Stanford University Press, 1974). Judith M. Bardwick, *Psychology of Women* (New York: Harper and Row, 1971), hereafter referred to as *Bardwick*; and *Readings on the Psychology of Women* (New York: Harper and Row, 1972), hereafter referred to as *B.R.*

4. Paul H. Mussen, "Early Sex-Role Development," in David A. Goslin, ed., *Handbook of Socialization* (Chicago: Rand McNally, 1971), p. 708.

5. See, for instance, the tables (pp. 93 and 94) in which *Bardwick* has documented the results of various studies on sex differences in early childhood.

6. Jane Austen, *Pride and Prejudice*, 1818. Quoted in Hole and Levine, *Rebirth of Feminism*, p. 205.

7. Quoted in Hole and Levine, *Rebirth of Feminism*, p. 206.

8. Alice S. Rossi, "Equality between the Sexes," in ed. R. Lifton, *The Woman in America* (Boston: Houghton Mifflin, the Daedalus Library, 1964), p. 111.

9. Cf. Lois W. Hoffman, "Effects of Maternal Employment on Children," in ed. M.S. Sussman, *Sourcebook of Marriage and the Family* (Boston: Houghton Mifflin, 1963), p. 242.

10. B. Bettelheim, "Women: Emancipation Is Still to Come," *The New Republic*, Fiftieth anniversary issue, 1964.

11. *Bardwick*, p. 202.

12. Erick Gronseth, "The Breadwinner Trap," in *Future*.

13. In Tanner and Inhelder, *Childhood Genesis of Sex Differences*, pp. 43 and 44.

14. L. Tiger and J. Shepher, *Women in the Kibbutz* (New York: Harcourt, Brace, Jovanovich, 1975).

15. For a discussion of the authors' biologistic approach, cf. John Archer, "Biological Explanations of Psychological Sex Differences," in B. Lloyd and J. Archer, *Exploring Sex Differences* (London and New York: Academic Press, 1976). From a historical point of view, Ann Oakley has shown in her excellent book that biogrammar has shown up in a country like Britain only 150 years ago! [*Woman's Work*, Pantheon Books, New York, 1974]

16. Cf. N. Cohen, "The Veteran Woman Member," *Hedim*, no. 89 (1968). H.

17. Y. Ron-Polani, *Until Here* (Tel Aviv: Am Oved, 1971), p. 97. H.

18. Lilia Bassevich, "Privilege of the Founders," in *The Book of Ein Harod* (Tel Aviv: Kibbutz Meuchad Publishing House, 1973). H.

19. Tiger and Shepher, *Women in the Kibbutz*, pp. 98, 146.

20. Menachem Rosner, *Changes in the Conception of Women's Equality in the Kibbutz* (The Institute of Research on Kibbutz Society, 1969). H. Hereafter

21. Tiger and Shepher, *Women in the Kibbutz*, p. 111.

22. It was printed later in Menachem Gerson, "The Adolescent Girl in the Kibbutz," in *Essays on Kibbutz Education* (Tel Aviv: Sifriat Poalim, 1968). H.

23. Rosner, *Changes*.

24. A.I. Rossi, "The Roots of Ambivalence in American Women," in *B.R.*, p. 125.

25. Olof Palme, "The Emancipation of Man," in Howe, *The Future of the Family*, 1972.

26. A book like A.J. Kaplan and J.P. Bean, *Beyond Sex Role Stereotypes* (Boston: Little, Brown, 1976) might help to do away with prejudice.

4 The Family in the Kibbutz

Over the past hundred years, the structure and functions of the modern European and American family have undergone a fundamental change, a change so great that a radical reformation of family structure is seen as inevitable and its future existence even occasionally questioned. Whereas once family life was concerned with the fulfillment of objective functions, now its main interest lies in the satisfaction of individual needs. This change has been defined well by E.W. Burgess, Locke, and Thomes,[1] who see the structure of the family as in a state of transition from that of institution to that of a voluntary group established for purposes of companionship. In this new form of family life, great emphasis is placed on the value of love, of emotional and spiritual incentive, and of individual happiness: it becomes important to foster the personality development of every member in the family.[2] There is growing appreciation of the fact that such a change can be brought about only as a result of far-reaching adjustments in the status and role of the female marriage partner. An extreme form of change was developed by certain communes: they regarded the family solely as an obstacle on the road to brotherhood and as a source of jealousy and tension.[3] These communes took the children from their parents and raised them communally, only allowing the parents to meet the children in a group setting and not individually.

For a long time, outside observers assumed that the kibbutz, too, was trying to rebel against the established form of the nuclear family and was even going to the extremes of these communes in trying to do away with family life. This view is simply not borne out by the facts. It is true to say that in the early days of the kibbutz, there were strong antifamilistic tendencies, but they were directed toward a control of practical family tasks and not toward the severance of the emotional ties which bind parents and children.

The approach to parent-child relations which prevailed in the kibbutz movement was established in the early 1920s at a time when the kibbutz movement was still young and most members were still single. It was a time of introspection and questioning of the family as agents of the old bourgeois order, which had been resented and rejected by the new pioneers, and of an overwhelming desire to build a different, better type of society. At this time, a veteran member of Degania, David Schmetterling, produced an article in which he examined the problems which face the kibbutz with the birth of the first children.[4] He asked if the parents are likely to regress to a private way of life, preferring an isolated existence in an enclave of domesticity and relating to

45

their children as to a form of private property. Schmetterling concludes that there is no reason why the powerful, intimate, and valued emotions between parent and child should be suppressed. In his opinion they are in no way a regression, in no way an expression of the desire to have personal possessions. To renounce the parental bond, according to Schmetterling, would be to initiate a falsehood alien to the human spirit. There were times when contact between parents and children was regulated and curtailed, especially in Kibbutz Artzi, but after a transition period, it was Schmetterling's approach which was accepted by the kibbutz movement.

Although the family has remained the unit par excellence, within the kibbutz framework suspicion and fear of its Philistine influence, which might ultimately strangle the commune, have been frequently voiced. This approach has been interpreted by a number of psychologists (Spiro, Bettelheim) as a rebellion against the Jewish *shtetl*, the small-town Jewish communities of Eastern Europe, and explained as an irrational "reaction formation" in the Freudian sense. We disagree with the latter interpretation for two reasons. First, only part of the founder generation came from the typical small town in Eastern Europe where Jews were in the majority and where they lived their own lives, segregated from the Gentile community. Warshaw and Odessa, not to mention Berlin, were certainly far from being *shtetles*. Second, the psychological term "reaction formation" emphasizes the irrational, compulsory, and unconscious character of a reaction. This was not the character of the famous "rebellion of sons" in the youth movement which had a solid ideological basis. It cannot, thus, be "reduced" to the status of a rebellion which stemmed from unconscious motives because, in fact, it was based on a new and distinct set of values, consciously adopted. In the *shtetl*, solidarity was based on kinship ties and on the continuity of tradition. In such a situation, intergenerational loyalties could be preserved. But this situation changed fundamentally when the youth movement exchanged natural kinship for a new form of solidarity, one founded on identification with a common mission and a unifying ideology.[5] Without this ideological basis, the young chalutzim could never have broken away from their traditional environment. To forsake their parents in order to establish a kibbutz in far-off Palestine became feasible only because family loyalties were subordinated to the sense of allegiance the future members of the kibbutz felt to their young comrades. The new relationship, the warmth between comrades, was increased by the feeling that they were to share in the experience of a lifetime, the chance to build a socialist community and at the same time to serve the principal need of the Jewish people. Small wonder that in this atmosphere community needs took absolute preference over kinship obligations and productive work took preference over domestic needs. In the kibbutz breast feeding was, thus, simply registered as "nonwork" in the work lists[6] of the time. Accordingly, even in the 1930s, as relationships within the group continued to be all-important, family ties were not demonstrated in public. I remember that at my kibbutz, most of the meals were not shared by husband and wife; nor did they sit together at the weekly assembly. Any demonstration of emotional closeness between couples was scornfully derided as a sign of middle-class morality. The birthrate was very low. It is hard to say whether this was in the main an outcome of the arduous living conditions or the expression of a certain reluctance about family life. In this atmosphere, marriage was regarded as a purely personal matter which officially hardly concerned the community as a whole. Close personal friends might seek to tender advice in situations of personal crisis, but the community and its organs refrained from bringing up for discussion even so grave a problem as the frequency of divorce. When the interruption of love relations manifested itself in the separation of a couple, the community felt it had no right to interfere. Similarly, since marriage was considered a purely personal issue between the parties concerned, no public wedding ceremonies, in which the whole kibbutz participated, were arranged. This practice continued even into the 1940s. Such an attitude, which resulted in the passing unnoticed and unnoted of a central event in the life of an individual, is now considered unfortunate by many veteran members who today regard this as a personal loss. Despite some feelings of ambivalence toward the family, especially in the early days of the kibbutz movement, no attempt has ever been made to sever the ties which bind parent and child. Unlike the forms of communal living to which we referred earlier, the vital importance of parental love for the child's mental health was recognized from the earliest days of the kibbutz. But the practical duties of parents and especially their prerogative in decision making on all matters concerning the child's development have been greatly curtailed.

A negative approach to the family such as is found in various communes could not be sustained in the kibbutz. As a voluntary socialist cell, dependent for its very existence on the identification of its members with its aims, the kibbutz could not disregard so vital a human need as the desire for family affiliation. However strong the antifamilial tendencies of the early enthusiasts, it soon became apparent to every one of them that relations among members even of a small-size kibbutz could not be a substitute for family ties. When the extreme hardship of the first few years had eased and the burden of bad living conditions alleviated, the child population grew considerably. Changes for the better helped the family to play a more conspicuous role in kibbutz life. When a proper dwelling with its own garden replaced the ramshackle tents and wooden huts which had previously been the home of the family, it provided a proper place for the enjoyment of leisure, for breakfast on Shabbat morning, for afternoon tea, and for meeting with friends.

The status of parents in the field of education has been greatly enhanced. Care is now taken to ensure that mothers of the younger age groups meet their children during working hours too. Regular consultation with parents of children at all age levels is now one of the duties of every kibbutz educator. The kibbutz family is no longer regarded with suspicion but has been accorded a place of honor in the kibbutz community. It is understood that stability in the family is a prime way of ensuring stability in kibbutz life. In the fully developed, older kibbutzim, the three-generation family is frequently found, unlike the situation in the city where it is rare to find grandparents, parents, and children living in close proximity. Most of these large families meet regularly. The individual family unit in the kibbutz makes its presence felt on many occasions, at public celebrations such as festivals and at private celebrations such as weddings. The family has developed such importance in everyday life that bachelors or childless couples may find their lot harder to bear in a kibbutz than in town.

Kibbutz Family and Modern Family

What are the specific features which distinguish the kibbutz family from other forms of modern family life? Three features are of a particular importance.

First, unlike most other forms of modern family life, the kibbutz family is not a self-interested economic unit. In its social structure, the kibbutz is not a federation of self-contained family units. Hence, the economic standard of a family in the kibbutz is not dependent on the endeavor and economic achievement and social outlook of the breadwinner or of the family but on the economic achievement and social outlook of the kibbutz as a whole. Although certain inequalities in the standard of living of members may exist, inequalities created as a result of gifts from relatives outside the kibbutz or by utilization of expense accounts attached to managerial positions in work outside the kibbutz, they are minor—sufficient sometimes to arouse ill feelings but not great enough to affect the equal status of members in the main areas of life.[a]

For the member of a kibbutz, the family is not the basic unit in the struggle for existence; every individual is directly affiliated to the kibbutz economy. This fact has important ramifications. In other family structures, the economic struggle constitutes a very real bond between all the members of the family, be the result the shared misery of failure or the shared elation of success. In its absence, the emotional and sexual ties between the spouses and their joint responsibility for the care of their children become the main guarantee of family stability.

There are two other results of the specific social structure of the kibbutz family. The wife is not economically dependent on the husband, nor are the children economically dependent on the parents. These two facts have brought about such a radical change in the structure of the kibbutz family that outside observers have sometimes called into question the very existence of a family in

---

[a]Restitutions from Germany have been the greatest threat to equality in the status of families, at least in some kibbutzim. In the great majority of kibbutzim, however, these monies were handed over to the common account.

the kibbutz; or if they have not wanted to take so extreme a stand, they have denied the family any vital function in the life of its members. Such a view of the kibbutz family ignores the facts; it stems from the inability of its propounders to recognize a type of modern family life different from what they are used to.

Second, unlike the situation which is found in other countries, where professional educators cooperate with parents mainly from the period of nursery school onwoard, in the kibbutz such cooperation exists from the very first days of the infant's life. The mother's share varies according to the age of the child. It is at its peak during the first year and diminishes gradually thereafter. The father is a full partner in the upbringing of the child from infancy onward. From the outset, the children live in the children's house, where everything is tailored according to the child's needs and capacities. The children's house is regarded not as a depository for the children of working mothers but, in every sense, as a home. Thus, kibbutz education has two emotional and organizational centers. Emotional content and practical arrangements are, of course, different at different ages. But cooperation of parents with professional educators exists at all levels and is meant to bring about a sharing of both influence and responsibility. In an ideal situation, both educator and parents listen carefully to the comments of the other. Needless to say, between human beings situations are not always ideal. Nevertheless, in kibbutz education the degree of cooperation sought and achieved is much closer and more interwoven than elsewhere. The task of the educator is not restricted here to a few hours of teaching. He (or, more usually, she) is in contact with the child for many hours and throughout varied activities. In addition, she is no stranger to the parental home because both educator and parents are members of the same kibbutz community.[b]

Third, the social framework of the kibbutz family is different from that of other modern family units. In the typical situation in the majority of non-proletarian families in the Western world, the husband works outside the home while the wife attends to household duties. Quite often, it is the husband who brings stories from his wider world to the family table, and it is the wife who listens to them. Such shared social contact as exists is often limited to interest in the children and to narrow family matters. As a result, the relationship between the spouses is impoverished. The situation of the kibbutz family is different. Both spouses live and work in the same social framework. The intense and all-embracing character of kibbutz life makes for a great number of shared concerns and much shared interest. Of course, there are great differences within the kibbutz between individual families. One family may look upon kibbutz life as being bound up with the great social and cultural changes of our time, while a second regards the kibbutz as a self-contained unit with its own problems, while

---

[b]Problems inherent in cooperation between parents and educators will be discussed in Chapter 6.

is very active in a specific area of kibbutz life (rarely the same for ¿and and wife), such as agriculture and industry, artistic activity or ñ, and a fourth may live a rather secluded life because psychological fac- ╱ not allow for active participation. In reality, there are many more than ╴mily types just enumerated. The onlooker too often forgets that kibbutz ╲bers and families differ individually just as people outside the kibbutz do. But the shared content for husband and wife which grows out of life in a kibbutz influences and enriches them both regardless of the family type to which they belong. The only exception is the case of the family which lives in seclusion. This family really gets the worst of both worlds. It has neither the benefit of involvement with life in a pulsating and innovative group nor the exigencies of economic struggle which in private families outside the kibbutz constitute a concern shared by both spouses. Indeed, in such families, only a narrow basis, on which the life of the partners can be built, remains.

In practice, the egalitarian marriage in the kibbutz has realized many features which modern family theorists declared ideal. Among other changes, both parents have a share in the upbringing of the children while at the same time economic independence is granted to all members of the family. There is, however, one important qualification. With all the undoubted benefits to the individual in kibbutz marriage, it must be stated that few women have been able to find for themselves a challenging and satisfying career. In addition, household tasks are in fact (though not in theory) regarded primarily as the duties of women. Therefore many women, especially those with young children, find it difficult to persist in activities which contribute to a continual development of their personalities. If they accept the status quo as an unalterable reality, they often become the main supporters of familistic tendencies in the kibbutz.

Until 1950, joint sleeping arrangements for the children in the children's house were the accepted practice in the three kibbutz federations. Only in four kibbutzim (three of them affiliated to Hever HaKvutzot) did sleeping arrangements for the children in the parents' home exist from the very beginning. To an outside observer, the thought of joint sleeping arrangements may arouse negative associations, including thoughts of separation from parents in the dark hours of night, connotations of institutional regimentation, etc.; but, as a matter of fact, these arrangements were an outcome of child-centered considerations, based primarily on the need to give the child maximum security and the best possible educational facilities. The solidly constructed children's house was built while the parents still lived in wooden huts or even in tents. This permanent dwelling for the child provided protection against harsh climate and defense against attack from Arab neighbors who were often hostile. As a matter of principle, joint sleeping arrangements were an integral part of a dual-centered educational system. It was only in 1950 that Hever HaKvutzot decided to allow transition to private sleeping arrangements in other kibbutzim too. Since then, the number of kibbutzim with private sleeping arrangements has grown, and it seems that this trend is expanding. While initially the trend has appeared only in Ichud, it has recently become a topic of debate in Kibbutz Meuchad as well.

There are few subjects in kibbutz life which have aroused such heated and repeated discussion as this problem. It may appear strange to the outside observer for whom the whole matter may seem no more than an organizational arrangement. But it is typical of kibbutz life that discussions on cardinal principles are frequently aroused by a practical organizational problem. The kibbutz is not an academic society for which perpetual and permanent clarification is its very life blood; the kibbutz is concerned with day-to-day realization of principles. Thus, in the main, a discussion of principles is brought about by a controversial, organizational proposal or in the wake of a controversial personal demand by one of its members.

The debates on sleeping arrangements in Ichud were followed up by research undertaken by the late Yonina Talmon, a sociologist from Hebrew University.[7] Her work revealed that far from being a merely organizational problem, the introduction of private sleeping arrangements for children in a kibbutz disclosed previously unobserved trends toward the implementation of familistic changes in the kibbutz. Talmon found that familistic and individualistic motives, as opposed to collective ones, were decisive in kibbutzim which had instituted private sleeping arrangements. Where private sleeping arrangements were instituted, the prevalent consideration was the benefit to parents and children; where joint sleeping arrangements were retained, the prime consideration was the benefit to the kibbutz.

Even more relevant was her finding that in kibbutzim with private sleeping arrangements, the emphasis on family concerns and on the achievement of a higher standard of living was much greater than in the other kibbutzim where greater emphasis was placed on the national and economic tasks to be fulfilled by the kibbutz. Talmon's results were first corroborated by research conducted by Shepher some twelve years later. Shepher finds notable differences among kibbutzim of the Ichud, differences which showed a clear correlation with the type of sleeping arrangements for children approved by the different kibbutzim. In kibbutzim which have adopted private sleeping arrangements, there is a tendency to increase the decision-making power of the family in the whole area of consumption. There is a tendency to eat the evening meal in the family home in preference to the communal dining hall.

Although, in general, apartments are allocated according to seniority, there is a tendency in these kibbutzim to strengthen the bond between branches of the extended family by having its members live in close proximity. The tendency toward strictly differential sex typing is stronger in this type of community, not only in the clear-cut division of functions between husband and wife at home but also in the election of women to committees. As a rule, the election of women to committees and managerial positions in fields which are not regarded as exclusive to women is unusual; but here it is particularly so. The presence of women at the weekly assembly of the kibbutz is lower here than in kibbutzim with joint sleeping arrangements. According to Shepher, all these phenomena do not appear only in the kibbutz which shows familistic tendencies, but they are significantly stronger in such kibbutzim. They restrict the possibility of social activity for both sexes but especially for women. Women also have to demand a reduction of working hours. The family's attention converges on their apartment and on family consumption.

In all kibbutzim, the privacy of the family and its active involvement in the upbringing of the children have been guaranteed. What characterizes the so-called familistic tendencies and makes them a qualitatively distinct trend is their supporters' demand for extension of the areas where the family has decision-making power and for preference to be given to familistic wishes and interests in any clash with communal values. Thus the prerogative of the kibbutz as a whole is receding. The change in priorities takes place gradually as more and more practical functions are transferred to the control of the family. A subtle shift in the ideological approach of the adherents of familistic thinking has become apparent. So far the influence of psychoanalysis has been great. The conflicts involved in the Oedipal situation were often quoted in order to demonstrate the psychological advantages of an education based upon two emotional centers. The dangers of fixation and overdependence of the child on the parents were expounded, with special emphasis placed on Freud's elucidation of the risks involved in the close proximity of the child to the parents' bedroom. Now suddenly all these insights, all these warnings, were cast overboard. In their place, there appeared a naive belief that the panacea for all the child's problems was closeness to the parents, especially during the dark hours of night.[c] This sudden change of opinion lacked a new theoretical basis. This was soon provided by a new emphasis put on the "natural." Supporters of familistic tendencies spoke of the "natural" tie between parents and children, of the "natural role" of women, of the "natural superiority" of parental influence over that provided by professional educators, etc. Little attention was given to the historical fact that this kind of emphasis in social matters on the natural has been frequently employed by conservative forces endeavoring to maintain the traditional order of society. They are not an appropriate philosophical basis for an innovative social movement like the kibbutz.

The view that psychological damage is done to the child by separation from the parents at night was shown to be untenable by S. Nagler,[8] a well-known clinical psychologist working in a guidance clinic of the kibbutz movement. Nagler was invited by the Ichud to lecture on the possible pathogenic effects of joint sleeping arrangements. In a lucid paper, Nagler reported that among the 1800 children who had by then been referred to the kibbutz clinic, he had

---

[c]It should be noted that no adolescent sleeps in his parents' home, even if younger children do so.

found next to no cases where common sleeping arrangements had been a pathogenic factor. He explained that where problems occurred, it was not the organizational arrangements that were at the root of nocturnal anxieties but the internal conflicts which the child sensed were affecting his parents, conflicts between the two personalities or created by their ambivalent approach to communal education. Where these conflicts existed, they were projected onto the institutional arrangements. Nagler also reminded his audience that the incidence of nocturnal anxiety was much greater outside the kibbutz.

Rational expositons of this kind, however, could not mitigate the strength of familistic trends, for in the main such trends are not a reaction to psychological problems (which occur in communal education just as they occur in every other form of education) but effects of social changes.

As in society generally, so in the kibbutz, with the increasing prosperity of a social group, the position of the family is strengthened. In the kibbutz familistic tendencies have been greatly encouraged by the consumer orientation which is typical of present-day capitalist societies, an attitude which looks on the raising of the standard of living as the "natural" trend of every family and as an aim worthy in itself. In her research, Yonina Talmon shows that familistic tendencies are greatly reinforced by consumer orientation; both share an orientation to the individual family as the sole center of life.[9]

Among all her other pertinent observations on familistic trends in the kibbutz, Talmon has shown that women in the kibbutz have stronger familistic leanings than men.[10] Here, she seems to touch on the crux of the matter. The frustrations of women, such as described in the preceding chapter, are the source of familistic tendencies. It is hard to imagine that a voluntary form of life can continue when the hopes of half of its population are not realized. To repeat a point made in Chapter 3, the alternatives facing the kibbutz movement today seem to be either essential changes both in the work allocated to women and in their position generally or a subscription to familistic tendencies as the accepted line of future development. The late Yehuda Messinger, a central figure among the educationalists of Ichud, said to me once in a private conversation: "Women have become estranged from the kibbutz. In order to win them back, we have to introduce private sleeping arrangements." This is a clear and honest presentation of one of the alternatives facing the kibbutz today.

Familistic tendencies have emerged with exceptional strength in the Ichud. For reasons linked with its history (see Chapter 1), the Ichud seems to be less impermeable than the other kibbutz federations to influence originating in Israeli society in general. This may explain why familistic tendencies are gaining so much strength here. Up to 1978, 67 out of the 88 kibbutzim of Ichud had introduced private sleeping arrangements; four others are discussing the problem. Among the 61 kibbutzim of Kibbutz Meuchad, there are 15 where the matter is under discussion or both forms exist side by side. Kibbutz Artzi is not committed to this line. All its kibbutzim maintain communal sleeping arrangements in accordance with a decision taken in 1971 at a large assembly of representatives of all its kibbutzim.

An addition cause of familistic tendencies, one nourished by deep emotional sources, is gradually gaining support. As early as 1956, Talmon discerned the renewed importance given to kinship ties in familistic thought. A large family is a safeguard against loneliness. It keeps parents from getting old before their time. The parents will not remain alone; their children will always be around them. Recent developments in the kibbutz have added considerable weight to her observation. The founder generation has reached old age, and the fear of loneliness has become a stronger element in their lives. In the process of growth, the kibbutz as a whole has lost the ability to be an intimate social cell in itself. As a result, the three-generation family now plays a vital role in the day-to-day life of the kibbutz. There cannot be any doubt that these facts have great existential weight. The issue, of which the question of sleeping arrangements is only an expression, is that of a fundamental change in kibbutz values and kibbutz structure. This debate cannot be settled solely through scientific fact finding. There is a sharp difference in the system of values adopted by the two sides. Personally, I consider the familistic solution to the problem of the kibbutz to be a regressive one, regressive from the following four different but interconnected points of view.

First, familistic tendencies are clearly correlated both to rigid differential sex typing and to a still further decline in the active participation of woman members in the communal life of the kibbutz. These changes are diametrically opposed to the changes we deem necessary in the position of women both in the kibbutz and elsewhere.

Second, further growth of familistic tendencies may do away with the most essential feature in the social structure of the kibbutz, namely, a family which is not an economic, self-interested unit in itself. This structure may be harmed by the trend toward a perpetual increase in the control of the family over its own financial behavior. If the extended family is allowed to operate as an organized pressure group in the kibbutz assembly in matters concerning vocational training and placement of one of its members, the result may easily be "hereditary" high-status positions of members of a specific clan. This would be incongruous with the kibbutz principle of equal educational opportunity for all members.

But there are already exceptions. There were a few kibbutzim which left the restitution monies from Germany to the families to which they had been granted, instead of pooling them. This has resulted in a conspicuous difference in the economic status of members and in the establishment of "rich" and "poor"' families in the same kibbutz. Similarly, in most kibbutzim today, members accept gifts from relatives who live outside the kibbutz. On the whole, these are small gifts which do not really upset the general level of economic equality. But if the family is in complete control of its budget and can choose its areas of consumption, it will be much easier to "augment" the family's financial resources through presents of considerable magnitude from well-to-do relatives. In a "familistic" kibbutz, this state of affairs may soon be regarded as "natural" and will thus be legalized.

All these minute processes, working in the same direction, in due course could transform the kibbutz into a different form of settlement, the communal moshav. In this form of communal organization, income is distributed equally among the families. The moshav lands and any industry it might have are run collectively, but separate households are maintained and women are recompensed by the community for the time spent in caring for their homes and children. In a recent piece of research on the situation of women in the cooperative moshav,[11] 61 percent of the women interviewed expressed satisfaction with their situation even though their conditions did not leave them any opportunity to engage in work of a prestigious or professional nature or to participate in the running of their community. Many members of cooperative moshavim were once members of kibbutzim, which they had left for a way of life which they felt would offer greater privacy. Thus, when the research team made various practical suggestions to the women on how to develop their interests and thereby extend the scope of their lives, the suggestions were rejected out of hand. Yet 90 percent of these women and 85 percent of the men strongly supported the notion that their daughters should obtain some kind of full, professional training, fearing that otherwise they might leave the communal moshav. It is easy to understand how in reviewing this contradiction, the authors of the article come to speak of "a situation of ideological trap." It is well known that this movement has remained small in Israel. This form of communal settlement lacks the appeal of the kibbutz movement, which represents a radical change in social life. Furthermore, since the life of the communal moshav is family-centered, it does not produce the strong drive toward activity outside its own framework which has till now characterized the kibbutz. In our discussion of familistic trends within the kibbutz movement, we maintained that they obscure certain cardinal features of kibbutz life. It is indicative of the development of these trends that in spite of structural differences, the kibbutz federation of the Ichud has recently decided to accept six communal moshavim into their ranks.

This issue is closely connected with another fundamental feature of kibbutz life. Both capitalism and the Soviet type of communism use the motive of personal (and, therefore, family) gain as the main incentive for work and economic achievement. The kibbutz has achieved its remarkable economic successes without this incentive. This is one of the outstanding contributions which the kibbutz has made to the solution of contemporary social problems. It should not be endangered by allowing the kibbutz family to assume a separate economic role.

Third, the kibbutz has emancipated its children from economic dependence on their parents. The important psychological results of this fact will be described in the next chapter. Suffice it to say here that any alteration in the economic structure of the kibbutz family would destroy the economic safeguard of this significant achievement and in many cases could restore the evils of an authoritative relationship, based on the economic dependence of children on parents.

Last but not least, a transformation of the kibbutz into a mere organizational frame of family cells would strike at the very human substance of the kibbutz. Talmon's research has shown that familistic tendencies were clearly correlated to a decline in the task-orientation of its members. In other words, the pioneering spirit of *chalutziut* was declining. Chalutziut should not be narrowly thought of as the ability to cope with demanding and primitive living conditions. The philosophical assumption underlying the concept of chalutziut (see Chapter 1) is that this kind of transcendence of a purely private way of life orientation not only enables the individual to become part of a great social undertaking but also rewards him with a measure of personal growth and self-realization. This reward is available to all. One should not assume that all members of the founder generation in the kibbutz were heroes and philosophers. Most were ordinary human beings whose lives had been elevated by the chance to overcome self-centered, narrow-minded attitudes in response to the demands of the task-oriented community in which they lived. The measure of personal dedication to this approach to life was different in different individuals and fluctuated in strength at different stages of life in the same individual. There could also be individual differences in the pattern that the task orientation took, because the kibbutz contains many areas of activity and needs many and varying talents and trades, the industrial worker as well as the nurse, the manager as well as the educationalist, the artist and agricultural worker, the politician and the builder. But there is one attribute shared by all of them—their lifelong dedication to a common task embodied in the kibbutz. This dedication has been the basis from which the kibbutz movement has drawn its strength, a basis which may be destroyed if the feeling grows that in the kibbutz as everywhere else, it is fully legitimate to orient one's life exclusively on the "natural" human concerns of family and on a constant effort to raise the standard of living.

Such tendencies can already be discerned in the kibbutz today, but their strength will grow immensely if, as elsewhere, they are recognized as the legitimate center of life. There is no dissension in today's kibbutz about the deep joy and security offered to the individual by happy family life. The controversy turns on whether family orientation should replace task orientation as the legitimate center of kibbutz life, whether the common tasks should be reduced to the level of a mere organizational framework. If the resolution of the controversy in the future results in a family-oriented organizational framework, not only will it impoverish the life of the individual member. It will also damage the influence of the kibbutz on Israeli society as a whole because the kibbutz will cease to represent the image of a new society, but will live in self-imposed seclusion.

It is impossible to predict the result of the continuing struggle on the content of kibbutz life. History does not know of any transition from one social regime to another without prolonged birth pangs. Both history and our own life experience can teach us that in such transitions a change of institutuions precedes the adaptation of the human mind to the new social system. Should we accordingly interpret the familistic tendencies as part of the process of change and development in the creation of a new social system, the kibbutz? Or do we see them as a stage in a process of disintegration such as occurred in numerous communes?

Since the kibbutz is a relatively small socialist cell within a large capitalist society, it is bound to be faced constantly with the need to struggle against the dominant value system of the larger part of the population and to reassert its own values. The result of the struggle will depend to large extent on the stand which the young kibbutz generation will take. There is no guarantee that the cardinal values of the kibbutz will be preserved. But, then, we are living in a period when the perpetuation of every value requires a struggle. Modern man has voluntarily left the paradise of religious faith and assuredness. But, as Buber said, the cause we are fighting for is too crucial to allow ourselves the luxury of either optimism or pessimism.

The Future of the Kibbutz Family

Many doubts exist today as to the future of the modern family outside the kibbutz, which has not only an emotional content but also an economic function. What of the future of the family in the kibbutz where family life is based exclusively on emotional ties? Maybe that future developments in the structure of the modern family as a whole could make this a problem significant not only for the kibbutz.

We shall attempt to answer questions on the stability of the kibbutz marriage on the basis of a survey of divorced families which the author carried out in 1963 within the kibbutz movement.[12] For our purposes, all forms of separation, both formal and de facto, have been included in the concept "divorce." Throughout the survey, we distinguished between the younger and older age groups. The younger age group comprised both kibbutz-born members, members of youth groups from the towns of Israel and from abroad sent to reinforce older kibbutzim, and the members of the kibbutzim which had been founded after the establishment of the state. The older age group included the first generation of kibbutzim founded before 1948. In including the more recently established kibbutzim in the younger age group, we were guided by two main considerations: first, most of their members were of a similar age to those born in the old kibbutzim; second, there are well-known differences between the two groups of kibbutzim, between those founded before and those founded after the state of Israel.

Kibbutzim of the religious movement were not included in the data because the problem of divorce in those kibbutzim is very different from that in the other three kibbutz movements. Among the 496 families from kibbutzim of the religious movement which were included in this survey, there were only three divorced couples. In order to understand this unusual situation, we turned to experienced members of religious kibbutzim and asked their opinion. They suggested that someone who had been educated from a very early age to forgo desires for the sake of religion would not even consider divorce as a possibility.

The survey included 10,425 families from the three large kibbutz federations. There were 877 divorced families among them, that is, 8.4 percent on average; 9.7 percent in the older group, 6 percent in the younger one.

The difference in frequency of divorce between the two groups emerges clearly. It could, of course, be claimed that in the course of time in the younger group the divorce rate would reach the same proportion as in the older group. We tested this assumption in a subsample of 21 kibbutzim (out of the general sample) which were established more than thirty five years ago. It seemed reasonable to assume that in these kibbutzim the oldest members of the younger age group would be concentrated. Our subsample included 1807 families of the older group and 977 families in the younger age group. The proportion of broken families in the older age group amounted to 10 percent and in the younger age group to 6 percent. This supports our conclusion that in the younger age group the rate of divorce is lower than in the older one. This result seems reasonable. Separation and remarriage with a new partner were especially common in the early years of kibbutz life. The difficulties of transition to a new country, to a new way of life, the lack of continuity and of tradition, distrust of the family— all these factors prevented the establishment of a stable family life among many members of the founder generation. Small wonder that divorce was frequent and that with the disappearance of these aggravating factors in the course of time the incidence of divorce became significantly lower.

We also examined the question of whether the kibbutz family is more or less prone to divorce when compared with the nonkibbutz family in Israel. Since our survey reflects the entire period, ranging from the earliest days of the kibbutzim until 1963, the measure which is normally applied in population research, the "divorce rate" (the number of divorces per year per 1000 adults), could not be used. Therefore, we had to turn to other statistical material. In 1959, the divorce rate in the kibbutz was 1.3 for women and 1.1 for men. In the same year, the corresponding figure for the population of Israel as a whole was 1.5 for both men and women. In 1951 the divorce rate was 1.4 for the kibbutzim as against 1.0 for the population of Israel as a whole and 1.5 for the town of Haifa. We compared the rates in the kibbutzim with those of Haifa because the population of this city was then more similar to the population of the kibbutzim in family structure, sociocultural elements, etc., than any sample which could have been taken from the Israeli population as a whole.[d]

We investigated the relation between the divorce rate and the duration of marriage. There is a widespread assumption that the incidence of divorce is particularly high during the first years of marriage with the logical corollary that there is greater stability after about ten years. There are, however, factors which operate as a deterrent to divorce outside the kibbutz, but which do not exist within its framework. In their absence, family stability could be threatened. Outside the kibbutz, divorce is much more difficult when there are children to be considered and when a certain economic status has been acquired, a state which is most likely to be found when the marriage has lasted ten years or more. In the kibbutz, however, neither economic considerations nor the presence of children necessarily acts as a deterrent to divorce or contributes to family stability. When we prepared our survey on divorce in the kibbutzim, we compared the material with statistical material covering the situation in Israel during nine years, under the aspect of divorce and family duration.[13] The comparison showed a relatively high stability of the kibbutz family—in spite of all the potentially counteracting factors just mentioned.

The presence of children in the family is acknowledged as a deterrent to divorce. There are three reasons for this influence. The first is the often extremely difficult economic problems raised by divorce in a family with children. The second is the problem of who has the right to educate the children after the break-up of the family. Sometimes this right is waived by both partners because each sees the children as an obstacle to the establishment of new relationships. The third factor is a psychological one. Many parents in modern society are aware of the psychological damage caused to the children of divorced parents, damage which manifests itself in the undermining of a sense of trust and security—the most valuable asset a child can obtain from a happy childhood where the individual feels secure in the love of those closest to him. Thus, for the sake of the children, many parents are discouraged from acting on the conclusions they draw from their ruined marital relationship.

In the kibbutz, the first of these reasons, the economic, simply does not exist. The support of the kibbutz child is assured even if his parents are divorced (as long as both parents remain in the kibbutz), since it is not the parents who bear the economic responsibility for the upbringing of the children. However,

---

[d]It should be remembered that among Jews from Arab countries and among Arabs the patriarchal family is still widespread and the divorce rate is low.

the other two factors, the educational and the psychological, do apply both in the kibbutz and outside it. With these factors in mind, a comparison of the divorce rate where children were involved in the kibbutz movement with that of the Israeli population at large reveals surprising differences. Of the 877 cases of divorce in our sample, 644 (75.6 percent) involved children at the time that the decision to divorce was made. In contrast, only 42.7 percent of the divorces in the Israeli population between the years 1951 and 1952 involved children.[14] Aside from the possible technical explanation that our questionnaire did not differentiate between the early period of kibbutz life when the divorce rate was very high and later periods, there seem to be two possible reasons for the surprising difference in numbers. The first is that the economic factor is a very powerful one; and when it is removed, the other two factors which inhibit divorce are considerably weakened. The second reason is that the psychological effect of the divorce seems less damaging to the child of kibbutz parents. They know that the child will not suffer such a drastic upheaval in his world because one center of his life, the children's house, will remain fixed and stable. It is, therefore, somewhat easier for kibbutz parents to seek a divorce.

Remarriage

Finally, we come to the question of remarriage after divorce. We deal here only with the social aspects, not the psychological ones. W. Goode[15] has described the social pressures on the middle-class divorcee in American society. In the kibbutz, the factors encouraging a divorcee to find a new family framework are different. Once again, the economic factor is not relevant. This is an important fact, for it frees human relations from many of their distortions and distresses. It reduces dependence on the partner and brings out the significant *personal* element in the relations between individuals.

At the same time, there are other factors in the kibbutz which make the family framework so essential that without it life is difficult, factors over and above the sexual drive, which acts in all social frameworks to encourage remarriage. Life for the single person is made particularly difficult in the kibbutz because there are fewer means of escape than in the city. Entertainment is more limited in the kibbutz than in big cities; so are opportunities to hide difficulties either from others or from oneself through anonymity. In the kibbutz, an individual is integrated by becoming a member of smaller social units where there are common interests or long hours spent together, such as the units which develop among members who work together or among immediate neighbors. Such groups are also created among the parents of children of similar ages growing up together in the children's houses. The single person is divested from regular contact with these mediating groups. At festivals, particularly, the divorcee feels most isolated and alienated since in most kibbutzim all celebrations center on the family as a basic unit. In addition, the educational factor, the desire to provide any child with a happy home where he will meet other children and recover from the effects of a broken home, operates in the kibbutz as well as in the city to encourage remarriage. In short, although some of the factors promoting remarriage are different in the kibbutz, pressure to remarry is certainly not weaker here than outside.

Table 4-1 shows the percentage of remarriages in the two age groups in our sample of 877 divorced kibbutz families. The fact that the proportion of remarriages is smaller in the younger than in the older age group is not surprising, in view of the fact that the former have simply had less time to re-form family relationships after what was probably a short previous marriage. It is interesting to note that whereas remarriage is more frequent among men than among women in the older age group, the opposite is true in the younger age group. An even more significant result shown in the table is the high overall proportion of remarriages, particularly of both partners. In the kibbutz sample it reached an average of 59.6, while in 1959, for instance, only 43.8 percent in the Israeli population remarried. There are limitations inherent in comparing the results of a single year to those of a number of years. However, this comparison can at least provide us with some basis for orientation. The proportion of kibbutz divorcees who remarry is apparently so high because there are no economic difficulties standing in the way of remarriage, while the social pressures we have just described serve to emphasize the vital importance of family life.

A Replication

The stability of the kibbutz family is of interest from the practical as well as the theoretical point of view. We decided, therefore, to undertake a replication of our survey on family stability. The replication was done in 1973, ten years after the first survey. For technical reasons we had to change our method, and as a re-

Table 4-1
Remarriages in the Kibbutz (*Percentages*)

		Remarried			
	Not Remarried	Men Only	Women Only	Both	Total
Younger Age Group	45.4	8.9	11.0	34.7	54.6
Older Age Group	38.7	9.6	6.2	45.5	61.3
Total	40.4	9.6	7.4	42.6	59.6

sult we could not gather material on *all* the questions included in the first survey. We also could not include the population of Kibbutz Meuchad. Our material did, however, comprise the *whole* population of the other two kibbutz federations; it also enabled us to have a look at two additional variables—kibbutz-born members as compared with others and the correlation between country of origin and incidence of divorce. Our report deals with the population of both kibbutz federations as one unit. We should also like to emphasize that this replication reflects not the whole period from the establishment of kibbutzim until 1963 (as in the first survey), but only the situation during the year 1973. In the replication we used three clearly defined age groups: 20 to 29, 30 to 49, and 50 plus. These differences in the organization of our material do not allow for a comparison of the two surveys in every detail. But the principal facts are comparable.

Table 4-2 shows family status in the three age groups. Bachelors are not included in the table. They amounted to 15.6 percent of the whole population investigated—over 12 percent of them belonged to the youngest age group.

The first fact to emerge from a comparison of the two surveys is the conspicuous difference in the percentage of divorces: it amounts here to 6.7 percent as against 8.4 percent in the 1963 survey. What does this difference indicate? The first survey covered a long time and included the stormy period of the foundation of the kibbutz. Even though one can assume that many members of the founder generation have passed away since the 1963 survey, the situation of the oldest age group (50 plus) is still much different from those of the other age groups: only 79.3 percent are married for the first time, as compared with 90.5 percent in the second and 98.3 percent in the third age group. Although the oldest age group includes 8 percent widowed, the difference of 9.1 percent of divorcees in the oldest age group as compared with 7.5 percent in the age group between 30 to 49 is a salient and significant fact. The oldest age group included only 22 kibbutz-born persons. Thus we may safely conclude that the replication has fully confirmed the result we arrived at in our first survey: the much greater stability of families in the younger age group, which was noted then, is not due to their young age which "has not given them time" to divorce. Our two surveys prove that the stability of the kibbutz family has grown conspicuously since the first two decades of kibbutz existence. This has been corroborated by another fact: while in the first survey the percentage of remarried couples among the divorcees reached 59.6 percent, in the 1973 survey it amounted to 72.4 percent (the percentage of women among those who remarried was slightly higher than that of men—38.3 percent as against 34.1 percent).

There are two other results of our replicated survey worthy of mention. One is the correlation between the country of origin and the incidence of divorce. This is shown in Table 4-3.[e] Hence purely individual elements are not the only

---

[e]The table shows how decisive Israel's contribution to the present kibbutz population is (thirty years ago the picture would have been quite different). It also shows how few immigrants from the Middle East or North African countries were attracted to the kibbutz movement.

Table 4-2
Family Status in Two Kibbutz Movements

Family Status	Ages	Numbers[a]				Percentages			
		20-29	*30-49*	*50+*	*Total*	*20-29*	*30-49*	*50+*	*Total*
1. First marriage		5,970	10,375	7,903	24,248	98.3	90.5	79.3	88.2
2. Second marriage after divorce		40	636	612	1,288	0.7	5.6	6.1	4.7
3. Second marriage after widowhood		3	118	359	480	0.0	1.0	3.6	1.7
4. Third marriage or more		1	12	34	47	0.0	0.1	0.4	0.2
5. Divorced		43	206	257	506	0.7	1.8	2.6	1.8
6. Widowed		17	110	799	926	0.3	1.0	8.0	3.4
Total		6,074	11,457	9,964	27,495	100	100	100	100

[a]The figures mentioned denote individuals, not couples.

Table 4-3
Kibbutz Population by Country of Origin and Incidence of Divorce

	Population		Divorcees	
	Percentage	*N*	*Percentage*	*N*
Israel	38.5	11,112	3.8	338
Eastern Europe	27.8	8,023	7.6	613
Central and Western Europe	13.0	3,760	11.7	441
United States and Canada	3.2	927	7.5	70
South America	6.6	1,901	5.4	102
Middle East and North Africa	4.6	1,317	6.3	83
Others	6.3	1,820	10.6	194
Totals	100.0	28,860	6.4	1,841

Note: The table does not include bachelors.

A comparison between the two outer columns of the table reveals the considerable differences in the frequency of divorce which exist in the kibbutz between immigrants from different countries. The results illustrate the influence of cultural background on the incidence of divorce even when the present environment is the same.

factors which determine divorce. One extreme is represented here by immigrants from the U.S. and Canada. The result concerning the Middle East countries seems surprising, but one should not forget that even though affiliation to a kibbutz is not made by the *most* tradition-minded people of this origin, even for *them* it brings about a far-reaching change in their life-style. The other extreme, i.e., family stability, is represented in our table by people from Israeli origin. Without an attempt here at an in-depth investigation, one fact immediately comes to mind as a possible explanation. People who were born and raised in Israel did not have to face the exigencies and crises which immigration to a new country always brings. Quite surprisingly and unintentionally, a basic truth of Zionism is brought out in this unassuming table.

A second quite surprising result is reached when we compare the incidence of divorce among *kibbutz-born* people with other *Israel-born persons and with the rest of* our population (again, without including bachelors). Table 4-4 reveals that kibbutz-born persons rate especially high in family stability, even when compared with other Israelis, a group with low incidence of divorce in itself. This is a significant result, but not an amazing one. It fits the whole tenor of our deliberations very well.

The facts show, then, that in contrast to widespread misconceptions, the family in the kibbutz shows a high degree of viability and stability. In the next chapter, we shall look more closely into the life of the family as we examine the relationship between parents and children, with special emphasis on the significance of the parental role in kibbutz living.

Table 4-4
Divorce among Kibbutz-Born and Others

	Population		Divorcees	
	Percentage	N	Percentage	N
Kibbutz-born	27.8	8,020	2.7	221
Israelis (not kibbutz-born)	10.7	3,092	3.8	117
Others	61.5	17,748	8.5	1,503
Totals	100.0	28,860	6.4	1,841

References

1. E.W. Burgess, J. Locke, and M.M. Thomes, *The Family from Institution to Companionship* (New York: American Book Co., 1963).

2. E.W. Burgess, "Educational, Cultural and Social Factors in Family Breakdown," *American J. Orthopsychiatry* 24 (1954).

3. R. Moss Kanter, *Commitment and Community* (Cambridge: Harvard University Press, 1972), pp. 13, 44, 90.

4. David Schmetterling, "The Family," in *The Kvutza* (Tel Aviv, 1925), pp. 103-105. H.

5. Y. Talmon, *Family and Community in the Kibbutz* (Cambridge: Harvard University Press, 1972), pp. 3-4.

6. Personal communication from Lilia Bassevitch (Ein Charod).

7. See Talmon, *Family and Community in the Kibbutz*. Her research was carried out in 1955 and 1956. In 1967, a second research on familistic trends in the kibbutz was completed by Joseph Shepher, a coworker of Talmon and a member of a kibbutz. See J. Shepher, "Familism and Social Structure: The Case of the Kibbutz," *Journal of Marriage and the Family*, 31, no. 3 (1969).

8. S. Nagler, "Are the Joint Sleeping Arrangements in the Children's House a Pathogenic Factor?" *Letters on Education of the Ichud* (Tel Aviv, 1967). H.

9. Talmon, *Family and Community in the Kibbutz*, p. 134.

10. Ibid., p. 59.

11. Dorit Padan Eisenstark and Helen Mayer-Hacker, "Women in the Moshav-Shitufi: A Situation of Ideological Trap," *Magamot* 21, no. 4 (August 1975), Jerusalem. H.

12. Menachem Gerson, "The Stability of the Kibbutz Family," in *Essays on Kibbutz Education* (Tel Aviv: Sifriat Poalim, 1968). H.

13. Cf. *Israel Statistical Abstracts*, 1962, pp. 59, 81.

14. Ibid.

15. W. Goode, *After Divorce* (Glencoe, Ill.: The Free Press, 1956).

5 Parents and Peers

Few aspects of kibbutz living have been so misunderstood by outside observers as those concerning parent-child relations. It is all so easy to make hasty judgments and rash generalizations based on limited observations. Howard Halpern[1] builds a theory based on one isolated incident: kibbutz parents want only the joys of child rearing and not the pains, they seek a role similar to that enjoyed by grandparents. In the same vein Bettelheim[2] describes the task of the parents as being only to provide fun.

A second reason for the recurrent misinterpretations is bound up with the innovative character of kibbutz upbringing. The unique features of this way of life are either misconstrued by the casual visitor or used as a basis for an attack by a theoretician who, all too often, has an ax to grind. At the beginning of Bettelheim's visit to Israel, a visit which provided him with the material for his book, he met with a group of kibbutz educationalists. In his impressive manner, he told us about his home for autistic children and explained that their rooms opened only from the inside, so that parents could not enter the rooms of their own accord. He added that he wanted to learn more about the kibbutz because here, too, the parents were not allowed to dabble in their children's education. Although his mistaken impression was immediately corrected, his erroneous assumptions were too deeply entrenched to lend themselves to real change.

Perhaps a third reason for the frequent misconceptions of the parental role in the kibbutz stems from the widely accepted notion that an exclusive relationship between mother and infant is the sole guarantee for the healthy, emotional growth of the child. The adherents of this idea are unaware of or refuse to accept Margaret Mead's conclusions based on cross-cultural studies. According to her research, it seems clear that adjustment is best if many friendly people care for the child.[3] Many people are inclined to idealize the mother-child relationship and to overlook how frustrating it may be for a mother to be locked up with an infant all day long.[4] What we are criticizing here is the orthodox approach which assumes uncritically that a children's house in the kibbutz is just an ameliorated version of the wretched institutions described by R. Spitz. Because parent-child relations in the kibbutz are really quite different in their structure from those which exist in the "normal" nuclear family, it is difficult for outsiders to grasp their nature. It seems to them that with children not economically dependent on their parents and not living under the same roof, with contact between parents and children only "intermittent" and with *metaplot* (care givers) "interfering" in the lives of the children from earliest age onward, it is "natural" for parent-child relations to become void of content and for parental influence to recede into the shadows.

It is difficult for everyone to get rid of a deeply rooted belief and cognitive fashion and to adopt an unprejudiced view of a new phenomenon. It is to Rabin's great credit that in his many publications about growing up in a kibbutz[5] he was the first to investigate the process of kibbutz upbringing in a systematic way. He compares it with the more traditional form of child rearing in the moshav and begins an analysis of the applicability of terms like *maternal deprivation* and *hospitalism* to kibbutz reality. It is no exaggeration to say that he put an end to the belief that hospitalism exists in the kibbutz.

Parents' Roles in Early Kibbutzim

It may be useful to start our discussion with a look at the role of parents in the earlier periods of the kibbutz movement. It will be interesting to see what changes have been introduced and how and why such changes were effected. One custom which until the 1930s certainly brought much distress to young mothers was widespread in kibbutzim (apparently in all three federations): a nursing mother was not only responsible for her own baby, but also had to nurse another infant if his mother did not have enough milk. This custom, which now seems absurd to kibbutz mothers, was the outcome of a radical interpretation of the principle of sharing everything. It was abandoned in the early 1940s.

Another extreme attitude, found then primarily in Kibbutz Artzi, resulted in the granting of almost absolute authority to *metaplot* working with infants. Since they were then the only *metaplot* who had received a year's training, they assumed the manner of the authoritative expert whose task it was to lay down obligatory rules for the laymen, i.e., the mothers. In the name of hygiene, on entering the infants' house, the parents not only had to wear a white apron, but also were made to feel as guests who had to adapt themselves to the rules of the infants' house. But this sort of extremism did not last long either. When in the early 1940s I went on behalf of the central educational committee of Kibbutz Artzi to my first lecture in a kibbutz, it was my task to speak against this system in which the monopolizing *metapelet* (caregiver) would not allow parents to participate in tasks such as spoon-feeding or bathing their infant. The main argument against the rigid restriction of parent-child contact was the fact that such contact adds greatly to the balanced emtional development of the child. Gradually, it was felt that the role of the parent in communal education had to be defined more precisely. On the one hand, it was generally agreed that parent-child contact was beneficial. On the other hand, the acceptance of Freudian psychological theories created fears that deep emotional involvement between parent and child in certain cases could have pathological consequences. Somehow a balance had to be achieved. It was finally decided that every effort should be made to help parents feel at home in the children's house, that they should be involved in all aspects of their child's upbringing, that they should enjoy maximum cooperation with all his instructors, but that the parents should not have the privilege of making decisions on matters concerning their own child.[6]

In this early period, it seemed all-important to bring about a reshaping of parental attitudes in order to forge a common approach to a common problem. Members of the founder generations had grown up in widely divergent educational climates. Some had come from a strictly authoritarian background, others from an easygoing upbringing which stressed that parents were the "natural" and ideal educators of the child; still others had grown up in intellectual circles where a laissez faire policy was regarded as the most modern and healthy way to raise a child.[a]

Although all the members of the kibbutz were overly enthusiastic about the new social experiment and its communal system of education, consciously or otherwise, they judged the new methods of child raising for good or bad according to the standards of their own background, in many cases rationalizing their position by quoting psychoanalytical theories of projection and transference. In order to ensure genuine acceptance of the new system of communal education, a *sine qua non* for its success, lectures were given and discussion groups were held, all directed at creating a common attitude. In Kibbutz Artzi, particularly, the task of clarification and then discussion and consensus of opinion was accorded special importance. In every case, it was agreed that the evasion of parental influence was not desirable; to avoid parental involvement was not in line with Freudian theory but a misrepresentation of it. On the other hand, it was contended that an authoritarian attitude, the pillar of class rule, was not becoming to a socialist, democratic community. In the early days of the kibbutz, such clarification and discussion contributed greatly to a better understanding of the system of communal education. Nowadays, when communal education is an established and accepted fact, such discussion is rarely needed. Where parents are ill at ease in the system, they are referred to one of the three kibbutz clinics which deal with child and family guidance or to the local mental health worker.

During all these changes and developments, the role of parents has always been conceived with the psychological needs of the parents in mind. Their role has never been defined as that of providing auxiliary support to safeguard the existing social system as it is, for example, in another form of dual-centered socialization system such as we find in Soviet Russia.[7] Soviet parents play an active part in the life of a school or day care center. But their tasks are meticulously defined by authoritative experts. The tasks of the parents' committee are mainly concerned with control of the parents' educational activity at home. In

---

[a]The inclinations of first-generation parents toward a laissez faire attitude in child rearing have frequently met strong disapproval in the second generation.

addition, parents' committees are obliged to circulate pedagogical propaganda among the parents and to assist the school in administrative tasks. It is obvious that the emphasis in this form of cooperation is neither on assistance to the individual child nor on a representation of the parents' views, but on the promotion of the official line of thought. This attitude to cooperation with parents is untenable in a voluntary community like the kibbutz.

One of the unique features of parent-child relations in the kibbutz results from the fact that the child is not economically dependent on the parents. The source of his economic security and well-being is the responsibility of the community as a whole, a social unit which is too large to allow the child to develop feelings of dependence, at least not before adolescence. How did it come about that founders of the kibbutz accorded their children a position so different from that in common practice? One reason was, of course, their craving for shared responsibility in every sphere. But there were additional motives. We have already referred to the reaction of the founder members to the authoritarian upbringing practiced by their parents. This was not the only source of contention between those two generations. Adherence to a youth movement, later to culminate in immigration to the Israel, often created a profound conflict of values. The founder members did not share their parents' respect for the importance of a personal career and economic success. Nor did they abandon their desire to emigrate to Israel in response to parental pressures. In many cases, this decision was taken with the disregard for the feelings and interests of the older generation, typical of many youngsters. But painful memories and feelings of guilt, which were at first suppressed, emerged later. It is no wonder that a kibbutz member, racked by memories of his own conflict-ridden youth, desired to give his child a happy and secure childhood.

In addition to the conscious desire of the kibbutz parent to give his child what he had frequently lacked as a youngster, a sense of freedom and trust in the world was prescribed both by modern educational thought and by the very structure of kibbutz society which negates the personal economic dependence of an individual on an employer. It was therefore completely fitting for the community as a whole (including bachelors) to make itself economically responsible for its children. The social and psychological results of this decision are far-reaching and manifold. The most obvious one is that the economic well-being of the children is secure even in cases of the death of the parents. Nor does care for the children impose a crushing obligation on one of the spouses after divorce. As a result, the absence of economic dependence of children on their parents has a profound effect on the whole parent-child relationship: parents cannot take this relationship for granted. When parents of young children have no time for their children or do not know what to do with them in the afternoon hours, they may have to face the fact that their child of 5 or 6 prefers to spend most of his free time with his peers or with warm and accepting parents of children from his group. There is no pressing need such as for food or pocket money to compel him to come regularly to his parents' apartment. Needless to say, the freedom to choose between close contact with parents or limited contact grows considerably during adolescence. I do not assume that kibbutz parents are consciously motivated by this cognition. But it is a fact that there is no cruelty to children in the kibbutz and that public opinion in the kibbutz is quite intolerant toward a case of overt neglect by parents.

But it is not only within the nuclear family that the child's sense of security is developed. Within the kibbutz, he grows in an atmosphere of trust and confidence; he learns that not only his parents but almost every adult he meets is friendly and helpful. Later in this chapter, we shall also deal with some of the problems engendered by this friendly atmosphere.

The absence of economic dependence also frees the adolescent or young adult from economic considerations when he forms his own value system, chooses an occupation or a sexual partner. Parents can be only as influential as the personal relationship allows. Parental wishes or whims cannot be imposed by economic pressure.

We are, of course, aware of the fact that there are a growing number of sensible parents outside the kibbutz who would never resort to the application of economic pressure in their relationship with their sons and daughters. Still, the situation of kibbutz parents is different in two respects. First, public opinion here has a greater impact. Second, and perhaps more important, parental behavior in the kibbutz does not rest only on the personal views of a couple of parents; it is anchored and backed up by a social system which does not allow for the application of economic pressure, even in cases of severe conflict among parents and sons.

Parent-Child Relations in Today's Kibbutzim

We have made some general comments about the attitude of the kibbutz to the parental role, but the reader may well feel that he still has no clear picture of the way in which the parent-child relationship works in the kibbutz setting. It might be helpful, therefore, to trace the form of this relationship as we find it in most kibbutzim today.

During the last months of pregnancy, the *metapelet* who will work with the newborn child contacts the expectant mother (especially if she expects her first child) to talk with her about her problems and expectations and to invite her to the infant house in order to familiarize her with its arrangements. This contact initiates a close relationship between mother and *metapelet* which has now become an integral part of the caregiver's task. After giving birth, the young mother is relieved of work for six weeks. Food and laundry for children are arranged by the service branches of the kibbutz. Breast feeding is accepted practice. The period spent in nursing is not limited except by the mother's capacity to continue. After six weeks the young mother gradually starts work in the kibbutz again, her work schedule beginning with four hours. Until the end of the fifth month[b] all the meals are given by the mother even if she does not breast-feed. In the sixth month of the child's life one meal is provided by the *metapelet*. Gradually by the ninth month, the four main meals are all transferred to the *metapelet*'s care, while the mother continues to bottle-feed her child in the morning and evening. For every meal the mother has three-quarters of an hour or an hour at her disposal.

From the time the child is 8 months old, mothers get time off from work to be with him for an hour in the morning and at mdday. This free time is gradually shortened to half an hour. It continues until the child reaches the age of 2½. Fathers try their best to spend at least a short period every morning with their infant. Young kibbutz fathers are very much involved in their children's life and actively participate at the infant stage in functions such as bottle-feeding and diapering. Apart from kibbutzim with private sleeping arrangements, the kibbutz child spends most of his time with his peers in the children's house. In the afternoon, he spends three or four hours with his parents at their apartment, walking together in the kibbutz or in its vicinity, visiting other families, etc. On the Sabbath, children of all ages spend a great deal of time with their parents. The working day of kibbutz members is so organized that as a rule both parents are able to be with their children during afternoon hours. Both children and parents reserve these hours for their meeting. It is this carefree daily meeting attended by both mother and father which provides the main basis for parent-child relations in the kibbutz. As soon as he starts walking and is able to get around on his own, a kibbutz toddler also sees his parents while they work. Visits with the parents at their place of work are encouraged from an early age onward, and the child can be sure of being a welcome guest. Toddlers at the age of 2 roam around the kibbutz on their own, taking it for granted that every adult they meet will help them when they lose their way or are in difficulty. Thus they develop a sense of basic trust in their relation to the adult world.

It would be erroneous to assume that the approach of kibbutz children to their social environment is shaped only in the children's house where they spend most of their time. Small children also spontaneously absorb the social approach of their parents during their afternoon meetings. The "social style" of kibbutz parents, as in the world outside, is quite varied. Some parents prefer to stay in their apartment or to keep to themselves while sitting on a lawn, even though other families are present. Others take for granted an easygoing course of interaction among all the adults and children present on the lawn. Needless to say, the effect of parental attitudes is felt in all spheres. Different parents respond in

---

[b]There are, of course, local variations of the arrangements described. For instance, in many kibbutzim today parents are free to decide by themselves whether they want to have their newborn child stay in their apartment for the first six weeks.

different ways to the child's questions, thereby either stimulating or stifling his curiosity and interest. Similarly, the response of the parents to the adults in their social environment will leave its mark on the child.

From his earliest days onward, the kibbutz child grows up in a group of peers. This is perhaps the most unique aspect of socialization in the kibbutz. It is unfortunate that so far this aspect has not been studied in a systematic way. There are quite a few theoretical statements about the vital importance of the peer group at the infant stage. They emphasize that the existence of a peer group from birth onward grants the child a feeling of belonging which strengthens his self-confidence. Or they point to the fact that for the small child, life in a group of peers prevents regression into passivity and autoeroticism. But these statements have a rather speculative character and cannot claim a factual basis.

There is, of course, a wealth of anecdotal and impressionistic material on the profound positive influence of the peer group in the infant age group, well known to every participant observer: the joyous greeting exchanged by two toddlers from the same group when they meet by chance in the afternoon; the contacts made among infants of 6 months, shown in several films; the concern about the absence of one of the children when the group sets out for a joint activity; the help given by a strong child (who at other times may be quite aggressive) to his peers against a threatening dog or an older child; and so on. Although such material has not been scientifically examined, it does give a general impression of the positive influence of the peer group during the infant stage. We should, however, point out that a large-scale research on peer influence at the age of 12, conducted by Uri Bronfenbrenner and his associates in twenty-nine kibbutzim, has emphasized a number of negative aspects, in comparison with that of towns. While both kibbutz parents and teachers were found to be much more supportive than their counterparts in the city, this was not the case concerning peers. The influence of peers in the kibbutz at this age was found to be greater than in town in one area only, that of discipline and control. Punitive techniques such as threatening violence, withdrawing companionship, or acting in a cold and unfriendly way toward deviant behavior were found to be stronger in the kibbutz setting. This may be explained by the voluntary character of the peer group in the city. The authors themselves refer to Shapira and Madsen's research[9] which demonstrated that kibbutz children tend to be more cooperative and less competitive than urban children in Israel. In any case, we feel strongly that more research is needed before we can obtain a clear picture of the impact of the peer group on young children in the kibbutz.

We can list the main features of parent-child relations in the kibbutz during the early and middle childhood period.

(1) The social behavior of parents exercises great influence on the children. Any comparison of the role of the kibbutz parent with that of a grandparent in which there are no clear educational functions or responsibility is erroneous. In the kibbutz, as elsewhere, the individual interests and talents of parents vary,

and the child is bound to be drawn into and influenced by the activities of the parents' home. On the basis of rich clinical material, Kaffman[10] and Nagler[11] have shown that disturbed relatives in the kibbutz family far outnumber all other pathogenic influences, both in frequency and in severity.

Since conditions in children's houses and schools are equal for all the children, there are no "culturally deprived" children in the kibbutz. But Moshe and Sarah Smilanski have shown in their important research[12] that even under kibbutz conditions the number of years of schooling a father received has a clear bearing on the intellectual accomplishments of his children. A home with little conversation, story telling, music, etc., makes only a trifling contribution to the child's mental development, in the kibbutz as everywhere else. The compensating influence of the children's house is in such cases of special importance.

(2) Kibbutz children have a better chance to get a realistic, all-around picture of their parents, especially their fathers, than city children whose fathers, and sometimes mothers as well, work far away from home. (This, of course, holds for any child who grows up in a rural environment.) There are many communal activities such as celebrations and festivals, cultural activities, and the weekly assembly in which children participate at different stages in their lives. From an early age, children join in some festivities of their kibbutz, later they take part in its cultural activities, and in late adolescence, they attend the weekly assembly where many spheres of kibbutz life come up for discussion. They get a good chance to obtain a realistic view of their parents as active or passive participants in the civic life of the kibbutz.

(3) The bond between mother and child in the kibbutz is as close and real as that which is found in any society elsewhere. Nowadays the small kibbutz child meets his mother in the morning as well as in the evening. But it is not only the length of the time which matters; what is even more important is the quality of the hours spent together, in particular, the carefree atmosphere which is generated. In her observation of mother attachment of 3-year-olds in the kibbutz, Maccoby and Feldman[13] predicted that kibbutz children would prove to be less attached to their mothers than other children and would therefore be less disturbed by separation from her. Both assumptions were disproved by her experiment.

(4) In kibbutz conditions, the role of the father has also undergone a significant change. Since he is no longer the breadwinner in the kibbutz, he ceases to be the main representative of discipline and authority. Beginning from his child's earliest days he becomes a full partner in most of the nurturant functions which in other societies are left exclusively to mothers. Generally speaking, small children think of the kibbutz fathers as friends and companions, endowed with such special skills as the ability to build things and to drive cars and tractors.

(5) Even casual observers in the kibbutz notice that the very structure of parent-child relations accords to parents positive functions such as support and affection while discipline, duties, and punishment are in the main relegated to

metaplot.[c] Such a division of functions at an early age seems justified in the light of Kaffman's findings that among parents of kibbutz children referred to clinics, parental mistakes were much more frequent than among parents of "normal" children. Thus, there is a possibility that the same system of child rearing which contributes so much to the mental hygiene of "normal" parent-child relations aggravates the problems of neurotic parents. In the kibbutz situation they cannot draw on any authoritative power given to them. The relationship to their children can be based only on the strength of personality, a fact which may increase their anxieties. In spite of these specific problems, we are confident that in general the dangers to the child's autonomy caused by parental overcontrol and overprotection are minimized by the existence of the children's house, which provides the child with a valuable chance to develop autonomy.

On reading my deliberations on familistic trends (Chapter 4), an American friend asked me why a mother's needs in the kibbutz are not always satisfied to the full. He asked whether there was an inherent conflict between maternal needs and the interests of the kibbutz. Our reply is that friction and dissatisfaction are not general, built-in problems of child rearing in the kibbutz. They appear in two instances—when the *metapelet* is not up to her task (and it is easier to replace her than to replace a neurotic mother) and when a mother is not capable of recognizing the advantages inherent in a dual-centered form of child rearing and feels a compulsion to monopolize her child.

The new form of parent-child relationship in the kibbutz is seen to be conducive to mental health. It is one which has to be understood sui generis and not through the ready typing of parents by such catch phrases as "grandparents" or "people alienated from parenthood."

Adolescence

We have already referred briefly to the influence of the parents and of the peer group on the growing child within a kibbutz setting. The time has now come to deal with the period of adolescence, a period in which the greatest change in parent-child relations occurs and in which the peer group exerts great influence. It will be useful, first, to describe the youth communities of Kibbutz Artzi, the first of the kibbutz federations to initiate a radical molding of new parent-child relations in adolescence.

In 1934 Kibbutz Artzi founded a youth community at Mishmar HaEmek, where the kibbutz-born children nearing adolescence from all the kibbutzim of Kibbutz Artzi were gathered. Since then there were very few kibbutz-born youth of this age group, they were joined by youngsters who had come from Europe.

---

[c]In Chapter 6 we shall see that this demarcation of functions is an oversimplification, at least as far as the *metaplot* of toddlers are concerned.

As far as both parents and peers were concerned, two principles governed the life of this children's community: distance from parents was considered to benefit the mental health needs of the growing child while the educational group, as it existed in the youth movement, was thought to answer the adolescent's main psychological needs. The adult educator of the group was expected to join completely in the life of his group and not restrict his activities to teaching. The educational setting and atmosphere of those early days were such that in his booklet, Edwin Samuel[14] does not even mention parents in his description of the various educational factors.[d] Youth communities of Kibbutz Artzi (rather unfortunately called "mossad," i.e., the educational institute) live on. Today there are nineteen scattered all over Israel. They have changed considerably since those early days, just as the youngsters brought up in them have changed. There are two main reasons for the change. Even at the very beginning, many parents did not resign themselves to the position on the sidelines provided for them by officially adopted educational theory. The other main factor which brought about considerable diversion from the original conception was a profound change in the educators: as they grew older and established their own families, they became unwilling to regard life with their group as the center of their existence. The change of heart which occurred within both kibbutz parents and educators as they grew older did not allow for the full realization of youth movement principles, such as the founding fathers of the youth communities of HaShomer HaTsair had originally intended. But the original impulse remained strong enough to prevent schools in Kibbutz Artzi from reverting to day schools, as in the other kibbutz federations, as far as adolescents are concerned (see Chapter 2). Study has not been accepted in Kibbutz Artzi as the only task which should govern the structure of a school for adolescents. A shared social life is regarded as an equally essential pillar of this type of school, and for the younger adolescents work is provided in the farm which belongs to the school. This blend of study, social activities, and physical work suits a boarding school which attempts to provide for all aspects of adolescent life.

In such a school, the *peer group* is expected to fulfill an essential role, much more so than in a school which caters to only half the child's day. This group is both a group for spending passtime and a social task group, a formal and informal group.[15] This group, comprising about twenty-five boys and girls, is designed to assist the adolescent in reaching emotional autonomy, closeness of relations between peers, and socialization toward study and work. There are, however, two problems which especially burden the mind of the educators, namely, the temptations of conformism and the capacity to form intimate personal relations.

---

[d]Y. Padan, one of the founders of this youth community, explains this omission by the fact that most of the parents did not live at Mishmar HaEmek; there were no regular daily meetings. Group meetings of parents with their children were organized from time to time. (Personal communication)

For its own sake, every kibbutz desires to raise an open-minded type of person who is endowed with a full capacity for genuine personal relations. It is not an easy task to achieve this aim in comparatively unified and confined surroundings. It speaks for Bettelheim's great perceptiveness that he was able to discern this problem during a short-visit to a kibbutz.[16] It is distressing that he has marred his accomplishment by a long list of hasty generalizations not borne out by facts. Such generalizations include denying the parents in the kibbutz any substantial influence and presenting a theory that adolescents in the kibbutz are fatigued and listless through severe sexual repression. Speaking about conformity to the group, he goes so far as to deny the very existence of a personal ego of the group members and allows only for a "collective ego"—a term I have found so far applied only to preindividual tribal societies. Bettelheim seems to suggest that the inclination of every adolescent to behave like his peers is taken in the kibbutz to such extremes that it impedes the realization of autonomy, the aim par excellence in adolescent development. In his opinion, intellectual development of kibbutz adolescents is impeded because they do not dare to voice a personal opinion that differs from the group's or to express themselves in a piece of creative writing. Bettelheim explains that they feel too weak to survive when their identification with the group is endangered (p. 262). A twosome is regarded as an affront to the spirit of the group which it actively attempts to break up by intrigues (p. 234).

The question of group conformity cannot be properly answered either by speculation or by the casual impressions of a short-time visitor. We have at our disposal two empirical sources which provide an answer. One is Alon's book based on a detailed questionnaire which was answered in 1971 by 130 eighteen-year-old boys and girls alike, who were brought up in one of the youth communities of Kibbutz Artzi. One of the questions deals with the climate of public opinion in the group and asks if it is tolerant or coercive. Of the respondents 30 percent said harsh criticism and pressure toward conformism were characteristic. 13 percent said that tolerance toward dissenting opinions and behavior was the rule, and 57 percent replied that public opinion was an influential factor in the group's life but no great pressure toward conformity was exerted on group members. This is a far cry from Bettelheim's simplifying generalizations.

Another empirical source which can be consulted on conformism in kibbutz peer groups is the large-scale research by Bronfenbrenner and his associates on the reactions of 12-year-old children to social pressure.[17] It was carried out in many countries and in different environments, including Soviet Russia, Israel in general, and the kibbutz in particular. The difference in the response of Russian and of kibbutz children both brought up, according to Bettelheim, where there was pressure toward conformism is very striking indeed. With Soviet children the highest deviation from accepted moral standards was recorded when they were told that neither parents nor peers would see their replies, whereas kibbutz children (and indeed Israeli children in general) under the same conditions gave the highest morally acceptable reply![e] It is just impossible to reconcile Bettelheim's allegations on conformism in kibbutz education with these facts. If these are the results concerning children at the age of 12, it seems reasonable to predict that during adolescence proper the autonomous view of the individual will carry even greater weight.

Is Bettelheim's picture of a collectivized robot, incapable of feelings of intimacy, a true picture? The replies to Alon's questionnaire show that 98 percent (!) of the group members felt lonely and detached at one time or another and were longing for company. When adolescents feel lonely, they seek a friend or a lover. Only 8 percent of the respondents said they had no friend; more than one-third found him in the group itself. Bettelheim has claimed that kibbutz youth are plagued by the effects of sexual repression. Yet Alon's questionnaire reveals that two-thirds of them began heterosexual relations at the age of 15 or 16 and most of them (84 percent) thought that in the last two grades full sexual relations could be included in the life of a couple who were going steady. An outspoken positive attitude to full sexual relations at the later stages of adolescence was also found by Nathan and Schnabel,[18] who did research on these problems in 1968 in the three kibbutz federations and replicated it five years later. The sample included 906 kibbutz-born youngsters. The positive attitude to full sexual relations was considerably higher at the replication: 93 percent of the boys and 89 percent of the girls approved of sexual relations on the basis of a love relationship; 27 percent of the boys and 48 percent of the girls favored sexual intercourse, irrespective of whether it was anchored in a love relationship; 50 percent of the boys and 57 percent of the girls reported that they had actually had sexual intercourse. All these results give the lie to Bettelheim's claim that kibbutz youth were sexually starved and plagued by repression.

In our refutation of Bettelheim's generalizations which we feel are unwarranted, we do not wish the reader to obtain an unrealistic picture of group life at adolescence, a picture of a life in which no problems exist. There was a time in the early period of kibbutzim when neither economic conditions nor the prevailing approach to communal upbringing allowed for an adequate measure of privacy and individualization, and even today the rooms where the adolescents live are rather crowded. Even after changes in conditions and educational approaches, for many an adolescent togetherness is still too much of a good thing. When members of the founder generation were 18 years old, group life was for them a dream to be realized in a far-off future. For the second or third generation it is their day-to-day reality, with all its small quibbles and minor problems and adjustments. They have learned that the atmosphere of the group is not completely governed by mutual trust, that backbiting and competition also play their part in group life.

---

[e]Bronfenbrenner's results as well as their rationale are much more variegated and stimulating than we can indicate in this framework.

I could give many personal impressions to illustrate the depth of attachment felt by kibbutz-born youth for all members of their group. Unfortunately, it is not uncommon in Israel to see emotions revealed as all the members of a kibbutz gather to mourn the premature death of one of its youngsters, all too often in battle. On such occasions, it is the friends, the members of the peer group, who speak openly of the youth who will not return, who tell of his attitude to studies, of his strengths and weaknesses, his hobbies, his feeling for life. They tell of youthful pranks, now related in public and relived as a stage in crystallizing adolescent group solidarity. No one who has ever witnessed such a gathering can fail to be impressed by the depth and the frank expression of feeling which characterizes the members of the peer group.

Early Research

In the mid-1950s Rabin[19] compared parent-child relations in a sample of 30 seventeen-year-olds in the kibbutz with 25 non-kibbutz adolescents of the same age, applying projective tests. Rabin found that kibbutz adolescents are less en-tangled affectively with members of their family and had fewer clashes with them than non-kibbutz adolescents (p. 179).

In a research carried out in 1955-1956 on the adolescent girl in the kib-butz,[20] I reached conclusions similar to Rabin's when dealing with parent-child relations in the kibbutz during adolescence. The sample included 767 girls, aged 14 to 18, from Kibbutz Artzi, Kibbutz Meuchad, moshav, and city girls who were members on kibbutz-oriented youth movements. The material is gathered from an anonymous questionnaire presented in a classroom situation.

From the replies some notable fact emerged. First, there are a particularly small percentage of girls in Kibbutz Artzi who rank the opinion of their mothers highly. Interestingly, this is not the case in the other kibbutz movement studied (Kibbutz Meuchad) where the percentage was far higher, apparently reflecting the stronger identification of the daughter with her mother. A second important fact emerging from the results is the high percentage of moshav-born girls who give greater weight to their mothers' opinions than to those of their fathers. This fact reflects the importance of the position of the wife and mother in the mo-shav family. The girls themselves emphasize the importance of her economic duties and of her household tasks. She is seen as the support who is always at hand, the educator and guide from infancy, in contrast to the father who is al-ways at work outside the home.

In the kibbutz sample, a considerable section of the girls deliberately em-phasizes that neither their mother's not their father's opinion carries much weight, thus expressing their wish to reach autonomy. Kibbutz-born girls, and particularly those of Kibbutz Artzi, express severe criticism of their mothers. The social-ideological education of these girls at this time emphasized an elevated image of woman as a fully fledged member of the kibbutz (see Chapter 3), and it is with this image in mind that in the research sample many girls level criticism against their mothers.

It appears that the attitude of adolescent girls to their parents was then largely determined by the extent to which the parents were active in the kibbutz and identified with the kibbutz and movement values. The subjects discussed with each of the parents were similar in the four sections of the sample: girls consulted their mothers about social relations, taste, and dress and their fathers about politics, economy, and science.

When girls were asked about the possibility of talking to the mother about personal problems, a continuum resulted with Kibbutz Artzi girls at the low end and moshav girls at the high end. The most interesting finding was the specification which appeared frequently in the kibbutz movements that their conversations with mother were "personal but not intimate" (in the questionnaire no proposals for replies were included). Girls giving this reply emphasize their excellent relationship with their mothers, a relationship based on friendship rather than authority which makes it possible to talk about many personal matters. They do, however, make the reservation that they do not usually discuss intimate problems with their mothers, problems such as those related to boyfriends or to their status in the group. They either keep these more intimate problems to themselves or discuss them only with a friend of the same age who could be of either sex. This response is given far less frequently by girls from a moshav.

It seems to us that the attitude to which we refer is not identical with the withdrawal from parents which is well known concerning adolescents. Withdrawal finds its expression in an unwillingness to spend much time with the parents, whereas in the average kibbutz situation the parents' flat does not lose its attractiveness for the adolescent. We assume that the attitude of "personal but not intimate" relations with the parents is connected with the emphasis kibbutz girls put on forming their own opinions which appeared frequently in the replies. The common factor seems to be a high achievement in independence, both emotional and intellectual, in their relation to parents. We also analyzed our material according to three age groups: 14, 15-16, and 17-18 years. The most telling difference between the four parts of the sample appeared in the oldest group: in Kibbutz Artzi there was a notable *increase* in the reply that personal talk was feasible (from 30 to 45 percent).

Methodological shortcomings of this early research do not allow us to give definite answers to some questions which arise from the differences in the development of girls in the two movements. There is no reason to assume that mothers in Kibbutz Artzi deserved stronger criticism from their daughters than mothers in Kibbutz Meuchad. We assume that the greater strength of the ideological factor in Kibbutz Artzi made its girls more critical and demanding toward their mothers. On the other hand, the growing closeness between mother and daughter which we have found with Kibbutz Artzi girls (especially in the oldest group) may stem from a growing acceptance of the reality of sex differentiation in work.

The attitude of moshav girls to their mothers is more easily understood. The whole family situation in the moshav is a more traditional one. Authority of the parents is thus questioned only later in adolescent development, and even then moshav girls are more reluctant to admit their criticism in replies to a questionnaire. The replies which the girls gave to questions concerning their feelings during the mother's pregnancy also throw light on the attitudes of girls brought up in different settings. See Table 5-1.

The high percentage of girls who "do not remember" is quite amazing, if one takes into account the emotional relevance of this event in the life of an older sister. Still, since in the majority of cases we had no other indication to go by, we had to accept these responses at their face value. But there were quite a few replies whose veracity was doubtful. The examples following may exemplify the basis for our assertion.

I had not special feelings during my mother's pregnancy. I was 11 then—and really didn't understand what was going on. I don't remember what my feelings were then. (15 year old, moshav)

We feel justified in classfying this sort of reply as denial, in the psychoanalytic sense of the term; oblivion is claimed in order to avoid the negative feelings aroused by the mother's pregnancy.

Another category which emerged from the replies to our questionnaire was "ambivalent feelings." An example follows.

Table 5-1
Daughters' Feelings during Their Mother's Pregnancy
(Percent)

Number of Respondents	Kibbutz Artzi (194)	Kibbutz Meuchad (145)	Moshav (84)
Does not remember	37	48.5	37
Happy expectation of a brother or sister	32.5	22	24
No emotional reaction	8	5	18
Jealousy	0.5	2	2.5
Anxiety for mother and child	2.5	3	—
Ambivalent feelings	10	9.5	8
Miscellaneous	2.5	3	3.5
No reply	7	7	7
Total	100%	100%	100%

When my mother was pregnant, I was embarassed to be with her. But at the same time I was happy to know that a brother or sister for me would be born (14 years old, Kibbutz Artzi)

With all the cautiousness due to the interpretation of the replies to a questionnaire, certain facts emerge clearly. The emphatic statements about the possibility of talking to mother about everything, given by moshav girls, opposed to the more guarded replies by kibbutz girls, give the impression that relations are close in the moshav and distant in the kibbutz. This impression is strengthened by strong criticism of mothers, voiced especially by girls from Kibbutz Artzi. Yet the analysis of the development of mother-daughter relations at different ages arouses doubt as to the validity of this concept. These doubts are confirmed and deepened by a study of the emotional reactions of daughters on their mothers' pregnancy. The "distant and critical" Kibbutz Artzi girls were the highest in happy expectation of a sibling and, together with girls from Kibbutz Meuchad, in their concern for the well-being of the pregnant mother, as well as in the admitted feelings of jealousy. On the other hand, moshav girls, apparently so close to their mothers, were the highest in "denial," high in their feelings of jealousy, and low in their expression of concern for the pregnant mother. This finding is at one with the expressions of growing distance from the mother as moshav girls grow older.

There seems to be more hidden tension in mother-daughter relations in the Moshav than the responses of moshav girls to our question on personal conversations with their mother indicated, probably because the family unit in the moshav is close to the usual form of nuclear family in two important aspects. First, the child is economically dependent on the parents. Second, the parents are the only center of care and love for the small child: the mother's role here is particularly prominent for she is the permanent companion of the child, especially during the early years.

Concerning the kibbutz, we have referred to the absence of economic dependence of the child on the parents and to the dual-centered educational system. These conditions enable kibbutz adolescents to express criticism of their parents and their opinions, thereby avoiding the dangers involved in the denial of negative feelings.

Parents and Teens—An Updated Research

The time has now come to deal with the influence parents and peers exert today in the kibbutz during adolescence. Among American psychologists there are widely divergent views about the division of influence between parents and peers during adolescence.[21] According to Ausubel,[22] by creating a new frame of reference, the peer group facilitates the emancipation of the adolescent from adult

standards and authority. Coleman[23] even speaks of a particular adolescent society in which most of the important interactions occur within the group. In
Coleman's view, loyalty and emotional ties to parents are replaced here by those
to the peer group. According to Campbell,[24] however, parental influence is not
reduced by the increasing amount of time the adolescent gives to commitments
outside his house.

What has kibbutz experience to contribute to this scientific controversy? In
1973 we conducted a large-scale research on the relations among kibbutz adolescents, their parents, and their peers.[f] We focused our interest on three main
topics:

1. The division of influence between parents and peers
2. The nature of parent-child relations
3. The variations resulting from differences in sex, age, and familistic orientation.

Our sample of 330 adolescents (57 percent of them girls) comprised two age
groups (14 and 17 years old). It was drawn in equal numbers from the three kibbutz federations and from those kibbutzim with private sleeping arrangements.[g]
We were able to reach 388 respondents among the parents of our adolescents
and gave them a similar, but shortened, questionnaire. The results of the two
questionnaires enabled us to analyze the similarities and differences in the views
of adolescents in a classroom situation and to parents in group meetings arranged
at the own kibbutz. The layout of the questionnaire allowed for the marking of
father, mother, both parents, boys in the peer group, girls in the peer group, and
the peer group as a whole. The answers to the various questions posed in any
given area were analyzed as one unit after the existence of high correlations
between them had been established. The tables present the results obtained from
the whole sample. The percentages for boys and for girls were calculated separately throughout the research. The total of the parents and the total of the
group together constitute 100 percent.

We mentioned earlier that children of all ages in the kibbutz spend much of
their time with their peers. This is especially true of those adolescents who live
in the youth communities of Kibbutz Artzi. We were interested in ascertaining if
adolescents are content with the way their time is divided between parents and

---

[f]I wish to express my gratitude to *Lotte Ramot* (Givat Brenner) who single-handedly col-
lected all the material in meetings with adolescents and their parents and steered the material through the various stages of statistical analysis. Without her unfailing devotion this
research would never have materialized. I also wish to thank Jehuda Asphormass (Tel Aviv
University) who was our statistical advisor and Professor Michaela Lifshitz (Haifa University) for her close cooperation during the important period of conceptualization. Professor
Lifshitz later applied two tests of her own to the sample.

[g]They are discontinued when the children reach adolescence.

peers. The replies to two questions on this matter showed the following results (see Table 5-2).

Our findings are quite surprising. In the Western world it is generally acknowledged that adolescents are increasingly eager to spend as much time as possible with their contemporaries while their desire to spend time with their parents is correspondingly reduced. We might expect that in the kibbutz, too, the parental role would be less significant, particularly since the children have separate living quarters. Yet our results show that most of the respondents feel that they spend too much time with their peers and not enough with their parents. Our table shows the average of the four sections in our sample. In the self-contained youth communities of Kibbutz Artzi we might expect a weakening of family bonds. Yet both boys and girls of Kibbutz Artzi are the highest in our sample (80 percent) to express their desire to spend more time with their parents. In the expression of the feeling that they get too much of the company of their peers, girls in Kibbutz Artzi are the highest ones in our whole sample (85 percent), while boys of Kibbutz Artzi in this respect remain below the average of the sample as a whole. It seems that boys benefit more from life in the closely knit peer group which exists in the youth community than girls. This finding contrasts sharply with the shadowy role outside observers have frequently ascribed to parents in the kibbutz.

Nearly a quarter of the respondents feel that they spend too much time with parents. It is notable that among those who feel this way, adolescents who have been raised in kibbutzim with private sleeping quarters are significantly above the sample average ($p = .05$): 27 percent of these boys and 29 percent of the girls reply that they spend too much time with their parents, a response which reflects a situation similar to that found in relations between parents and their adolescent children in Western society.

In our questionnaire we asked for an answer to the following two questions and for the completion of a statement: "Who knows you best? With whom can you express yourself most freely? It is most pleasant for me to spend my time

Table 5-2
Attitude toward Time Spent[a] with Parents and Peers
(Percent)

	Boys (n = 90)		Girls (n = 116)	
	Parents	Peers	Parents	Peers
Too much time with	21	79	23	77
Too little time with	65.6	34.4	70	31

[a]The adolescent respondents were asked to complete two statements:
"I have too much time to spend with . . ."
"I have too little time to spend with . . ."

with. . . ." We have summarized our results under the comprehensive heading Feelings of Ease (see Table 5-3).

These results corroborate the results of Table 5-1. They show again that relations between parents and their adolescent children are on average qualitatively different from those outside the kibbutz, where it is regarded as self-evident that the peer group is more attractive for the adolescent than the company of his parents. In the kibbutz, although youngsters feel a sense of ease in the company of both parents and peers, it is more pronounced in the company of parents. This holds true for girls even more than for boys. Another finding is that both boys and girls have a greater feeling of ease with parents of their own sex and with group members of their own sex, a fact which we shall meet in our research over and over.

It is generally agreed that in adolescence the youngster needs to assert his own personality and his growing sense of independence. Thus, it is taken for granted that frequent conflicts with parents are inevitable and have a more serious character than those of early and middle childhood. The type of conflict varies according to social conditions. For instance, in those conflicts typical of parent-child relations in contemporary American middle-class homes, Ausubel[25] lists the issues as control of money, automobile, and housekeys; parental interference in choice of friends; parental imposition of goals or violation of privacy. We are inclined to assume a priori that the absence of economic dependence of the kibbutz adolescent on his parents and the fact that he does not share his parents' apartment make most of Ausubel's reasons for conflict irrelevant to the kibbutz setting. In our questionnaire, we asked our respondents to mark three main causes of friction, first in their relations with their parents and then with their peers. Our questionnaire suggested twenty detailed causes. For the analysis of our material we devised seven comprehensive categories. We specify those which are not self-evident:

Table 5-3
Feelings of Ease
(Percent)

	Boys (n = 144)	*Girls (n = 182)*
With father	10.6	6.6
With mother	9.8	19.9
With parents	32.1	32.5
Total of parents	52.5	58.7
With boys in group	17.1	6.6
With girls in group	8.6	15.7
With whole group	21.8	19.0
Total of group	47.5	41.3

1. Differences in life-style comprised differences in dress and hairstyle, musical and artistic taste, insistence on listening to radio or watching television.
2. Avoidance of practical obligations including disregard for the property of others and refusal to serve on a committee of the group.
3. Status in the group expressed in the field of study, at work, and in sports or in competition for the position of favorite in the group.
4. School matters such as preparation of homework and evaluation of teachers (see Table 5-4).

By far the most frequent cause of friction with parents, for both boys and girls, is thus seen to be differences between the generations in life-style and in manners. Second come school matters which cause friction mainly with parents, again alike for both sexes. Avoidance of practical obligations appears in a different way for boys and girls: while boys meet this problem almost equally with parents and with their peer group, girls are more prepared to help the parents and have greater friction in this respect with their peers. The largest source of friction inside the group for both boys and girls is competition for status in the peer group in the various spheres detailed above; this factor is stronger for boys than for girls.

It was rather surprising to find that friction on the basis of different political opinions or different attitudes to issues in the kibbutz is greater with peers than with parents. Two questions immediately spring to mind. Do these results indicate that political and kibbutz matters have no place in the conversations the adolescent holds with his parents or do they suggest, perhaps, that the adolescent can deal with any political or kibbutz problem in a less emotionally charged atmosphere with his parents than with his peers? We shall soon take up these

Table 5-4
Causes of Friction with Parents and Group
(Percent)

	Boys		Girls	
	Parents	*Group*	*Parents*	*Group*
1. Differences in life-style and manners	35	18	37	20
2. Avoidance of practical obligations	21	20	17	23
3. Status in the group	8	24	7	19
4. Different opinions on political or kibbutz problems	11	18	11	18
5. School matters	20	10	20	10
6. Choosing friends and a mate	2	9	6	9
7. Parental pressure toward a certain occupation	3	1	2	1
Total	100%	100%	100%	100%

questions again on the basis of empirical findings. Parents' attempts to interfere in personal problems such as choosing a friend or a mate are a negligible cause of friction as far as the relations of boys with parents are concerned and a little more important in parent-daughter relations; but in both cases, friction on these grounds is greater in the group. The last result is indicative of the atmosphere generated by kibbutz upbringing: pressure exerted by parents on an adolescent to take up a specific occupation is negligible as a cause of friction. This is in keeping with our previous assertion that the quality of parent-child relations in the kibbutz is profoundly shaped by the absence of the child's economic dependence on his parents. In addition, as we mentioned before, the living conditions of the kibbutz adolescent are so different from those of his American counterpart that many of the sources of friction which we find listed in American studies have no meaning here, because parents and their adolescent children do not share an apartment. On the other hand, habits of domination and of restrictive, authoritarian, and interfering attitudes on the part of the parents cannot be engendered in a kibbutz setting.

Spheres of Influence

In the next part of our study, we were interested in seeing whose influence on the adolescent was greater and in which sphere. Our questions were designed to see if it is possible to differentiate clearly not only between those spheres in which either parents or members of a peer group exert the greater influence but also between the influence of mother and father and between that of peers of the same and of opposite sex.

In two areas—political opinion and sexual behavior—we asked the adolescent whose advice he would prefer if that given by his parents were contrary to that offered by his peers. See Table 5-5.

Table 5-5
Preference for Advice in Sexual Behavior[a] and Political Opinion
(Percent)

	Sexual Behavior		Political Opinion	
	Boys (n = 50)	Girls (n = 82)	Boys (n = 122)	Girls (n = 159)
Parents	8	35	44	51
Peers	72	45	25	19
Myself	20	20	31	30

[a]This question was not put to the 14-year-olds. Consequently, the number of respondents was comparatively small.

The category "myself" was not provided for in our questionnaire; the adolescents themselves devised this reply—a clear expression of their striving toward autonomy. The most striking fact revealed by the table is the decisive influence of the peer group on sexual behavior. Preference for the opinion of the group in this sphere is found with both boys and girls, although with girls reliance on the group is weaker. In the political sphere, willingness to accept parental advice is a well established fact, again more so for girls than for boys. Surprisingly in the political sphere the preference of the adolescent for his own independent opinion is more strongly expressed than in matters concerning sexual behavior. If the advice of parents on political matters is preferred to that of the peer group and is at the same time less friction-ridden, the logical conclusion seems to be that conversations between parents and their children on political matters mainly consist of imparting information and on weighing all aspects of the phenomena being discussed, while adolescents among themselves are more dogmatic and emotional in their mode of presenting arguments.[h]

We deliberately asked the same questions again using a different formulation. The spheres of influence concerned were now examined by several questions detailed in our questionnaire.

1. *School matters*: This included study, preparation of lessons, evaluation of teachers.
2. *Political issues*: attitudes toward Arabs in Israel, Arab terrorists who were arrested, Oriental Jews in Israel, new immigrants from Soviet Russia.
3. *Friendship and love*: choice of friends and a mate, sex information.
4. *Questions of approach to matters of principle*: appreciation of physical as compared with intellectual work; appreciation of women's intellectual ability; attitude toward full sexual relations during adolescence.
5. *Personal future*: choice of an occupation, service in the army, joining the kibbutz.

Our results show a clear-cut division of influence in two spheres: parents have the greater effect on the formation of political opinions while the group has the greater influence on matters pertaining to friendship and love. This is in full accord with the results mentioned above which were arrived at through a different formulation of the questions.

We investigated three other spheres of influence: school problems, questions of approach to matters of principle, and thoughts about the personal future of the adolescent. In all three spheres, parental influence was found to outweigh peer influence, although the latter remains a factor of considerable importance. See Table 5-6.

---

[h]This quiet imparting of political information in a tension-free discussion may not create an atmosphere conducive to future political involvement.

Table 5-6
Spheres of Influence[a]
(Percent)

		Father	Mother	Boys in the Group	Girls in the Group	
1.	School matters					
	Boys: $n = 425$	36	23	37	4	100%
	Girls: $n = 315$	18	34	4	44	100%
2.	Political opinions					
	Boys: $n = 191$	71	16	8	5	100%
	Girls: $n = 221$	86	12	–	2	100%
3.	Friendship and love					
	Boys: $n = 186$	8	17	69	6	100%
	Girls: $n = 294$	2	35	9	54	100%
4.	Questions of approach to matters of principle					
	Boys: $n = 129$	26	29	33	12	100%
	Girls: $n = 174$	14	54	10	22	100%
5.	My personal future[b]					
	Boys: $n = 61$	39	13	43	5	100%
	Girls: $n = 54$	46	28	–	26	100%

[a]The number of replies is high, because the respondents replied to the individual questions in every one of the five areas detailed above.
[b]This question was presented only to the older group; thus there were fewer replies.

So far, our examination has been directed in a general manner at the division of influence between parents and peers in the five areas investigated. On closer inspection, three more specific details can be obtained from this table.

In three of the areas, the majority of our respondents turn for advice to the parent of the same sex. This result is of special significance in the case of the mother whose influence on her daughter is not restricted to domestic or personal matters but also bears considerable weight in questions of principle such as the approach to physical and intellectual work, appreciation of woman's intellectual capacity, and the formation of attitude toward sexual behavior.

There is one area in which the influence of the father is decisive for boys and girls, but more for girls than for boys, namely, in the formation of opinions on political matters. In this respect, the traditional role of the father has not changed in the kibbutz.

Last but not least, because the proximity of boys and girls in the kibbutz is so great, one might expect the influence of the two sexes on one another to be strong. As a matter of fact, our material does not confirm this assumption. In all the five areas investigated, the main pattern of influence leads from girls to girls and from boys to boys.

Our findings do not support the widely held assumption that permanent proximity of parents to their children is beneficial to harmonious parent-child relations and conducive to the adolescents' willing acceptance of parental guidance. On the contrary, we have seen that when the child does not spend most of his time in the parental home, relations between parent and child are improved: friction is reduced while desire for the company of the parent is increased. Contrary to popular belief, conditions in the kibbutz have not denied parents the role of prime mentor in their child's upbringing. The kibbutz parent not only guides and influences the views of his adolescent child but also enjoys an easier, more tension-free relationship.

Our findings thus far seem to suggest that far from becoming parents without consequence, parents in the kibbutz play a major role in the life of their adolescent children. We were interested in examining further the nature of the relationship and the degree of influence exerted by father and mother.

Quality of Relations

We asked whether parents were overindulgent, leaving any demands on their children to be made by the peer group. The answers to this question were unequivocal; 75 percent of the boys and 60 percent of the girls said that it was the parents, not the peer group, who made the maximal number of demands. A complementary question dealt with the readiness of father and mother to take the initiative in educational matters in preference to noninterference in the lives of their children. See Table 5-7.

Our findings confirm that most of the youngsters do not think of their parents as overindulgent and both boys and girls ascribe to the mother less of an laissez faire approach than they do to the father. In the early days of the kibbutz, there was a tendency to grant complete freedom to the child, a tendency in accord with the the teachings of progressive education at the time. In judging according to the opinion of their adolescent children, this tendency has not entirely disappeared. Perhaps this is an essential characteristic of every nonauthoritarian educational system. In any case, the fact is that an undecided position in

Table 5-7

My Father (Mother) Does Not Like to Take the Initiative in Educational Matters. He (She) Regards It as Interference.
(Percent, n = 318)

	Father		Mother	
	Boys	*Girls*	*Boys*	*Girls*
Agree	36.5	21.4	26.1	16.4
Undecided	16.9	22	26.1	24.6
Disagree	46.3	56.6	47.8	59

the perception of the parents' guiding role is rather widespread: in the overall average of the sample, it amounts to 23 percent for both boys and girls.

In order to determine how the division of influence between father and mother is perceived by the adolescent, we included the following statement: "When I ask father a question, he often refers me to mother" (and vice versa). See Table 5-8.

The replies show that the fathers are more willing to state an opinion than the mothers. Or, to put it another way, the mothers refer questions much more frequently to fathers. Differences between boys and girls are small. As the high incidence of undecided replies (30.5 percent) shows, it was not an easy question to answer, and therefore we cannot jump to conclusions. As they stand, our findings show that under kibbutz conditions the strongest parental influence comes from the father, a finding which testifies to the absence of full equality between the sexes in the kibbutz and reveals the presence of a psychological barrier in the struggle toward its achievement.

Happy relations between parents and children should equip the child with a possession most valuable for his future life, namely, a feeling of basic trust toward life. This is achieved if from earliest infancy onward the child develops with a feeling of security in his parents' acceptance of him. But even in such a case, the changes and upheavals that occur so frequently in adolescence may undermine at least temporarily the adolescent's sense of assurance. In order to measure the adolescent's feelings of acceptance by his parents, we composed the following statement: "My father (mother) gives me the feeling that everything I do is important." See Table 5-9.

Almost 40 percent of our sample gave an affirmative reply to this statement. In the context of our other findings on parent-child relations, we are inclined to regard our findings as very positive, especially if we take into account that we are dealing with the period of adolescence. In any case, the most striking feature of our table is its consistency: there are few differences in the approach to father and mother; nor are there substantial differences between boys and girls. However, girls are less outspoken in their criticism of their parents' approach than boys; their part in the undecided section is consistently higher than the boys'. Perhaps this indicates that girls are more reluctant to voice criticism than boys.

Table 5-8
When I Ask Father Something, He Often Refers Me to Mother (and Vice Versa). (Percent, n = 317)

| | Father Refers to Mother | | | Mother Refers to Father | | |
	Agree	Disagree	Undecided	Agree	Disagree	Undecided
Boys	19.3	49.6	31.1	36.6	34.6	28.8
Girls	17.1	48.6	34.3	33.7	38.7	27.6

Table 5-9

My Parents Give Me the Feeling that Everything I Do Is Important[a]
(Percent, n = 317)

| | Father | | Mother | |
	Boys	Girls	Boys	Girls
Agree	38.5	38.1	39.1	39.7
Disagree	30.4	24.9	28.3	24.4
Undecided	31.1	37.0	32.6	35.9

[a]The border line between acceptance and overindulgence in the attitudes of parents is subtle and cannot be fully ascertained by means of a questionnaire.

In order to clarify still further the complex character of relations between parents and their adolescent children, we asked the adolescents which was the most admirable and which the most annoying trait of their parents, without giving any examples. In order to cope with the overwhelming variety of individual replies given, we arranged them in seven broad categories.[i] See Table 5-10.

Our table allows for the following conclusions:

(1) In the intellectual sphere, both boys and girls are impressed mainly by their fathers; in the work sphere, the sons have the greater admiration for the father.

(2) Our material makes it clear that the mother is the cardinal factor in the expressive sphere, in the interpersonal relations and in intrapsychic traits. This holds for both sexes (apart from the boys' evaluation of the intrapsychic traits of their parents), but to a greater degree for girls. Ambivalence exists in these areas for both boys and girls, but it is notably stronger with girls than with boys.

(3) Our results show that ambivalence is not consistently stronger toward the parent of the same sex. The various areas dealt with give different results and thus the classic picture of Oedipal relations does not emerge here.

(4) Practical aptitudes on the one hand and grievances on the other carry substantial weight in forming the general picture created by listing admirable and annoying traits, more so perhaps than one would have expected at the age of adolescence.

(5) The rank-order of the areas dealt with, considered from the point of view of their relative weight in the overall structure of parent-child relations, is similar for boys and girls. For both sexes, the personal-individual traits are high in the rank-order, while the attitudes of the parents to specific kibbutz values such as work and social ideals appear at the low end.

For the last question on the quality of parent-child relations at adolescence in the kibbutz, we used the sentence-completion method. The question to be

[i]They were proposed by Prof. Michaela Lifshitz.

Table 5-10
Admirable and Annoying Traits of Parents
(Percent)

| | Boys (n = 131) | | | | Girls (n = 164) | | | |
| | Admirable | | Annoying | | Admirable | | Annoying | |
Traits	Father	Mother	Father	Mother	Father	Mother	Father	Mother
1. Intrapsychic traits	20.6	19.7	28.8	30.4	23.8	26.4	31.5	21.2
2. Intellectual abilities	20.6	7.9	1	1	19.5	3.7	1.6	3.8
3. Interpersonal relations	13.0	20.5	24	28.4	25.6	31.9	25.8	31.8
4. Social ideals	6.9	0.8	2.9	2	4.3	1.8	1.6	0.8
5. Attitude to work and job	15.3	11.8	4.8	6.9	8.5	9.2	3.2	3.0
6. His (Her) relationship to me	16	21.2	20.2	23.5	12.8	21.5	25	28
7. Aptitudes and grievances	7.6	18.1	18.3	7.8	5.5	5.5	11.3	11.4
Total	100%	100%	100%	100%	100%	100%	100%	100%

completed was, "The idea that I shall live at the same place as my parents. . . ." In the sample 82 percent of the boys and 91 percent of the girls replied. See Table 5-11.

Apart from the old, tradition-oriented family, we could not expect to find that more than half the members of a young population would choose a place of residence simply because their parents were already living in the area. A second finding of interest is the difference between boys and girls, especially if we take into account the widespread opinion that girls are "naturally" more family-oriented than boys. In our sample, in any case, there were considerably fewer girls than boys who had a positive attitude to the prospect of living at the same place as their parents. One may speculate as to the thoughts which prompted these replies. Was it awareness of the possibility that the girl might need to follow a future husband to another area or an unwillingness to have parents nearby, who might interfere in the upbringing of future grandchildren? Was it a sense of frustration with kibbutz life? Among the replies which indicated a desire to live in the same place as the parents, three different attitudes were manifested. One, although positive, was aware of problems that might be incurred in this situation. "I don't think that I shall live at the same place, but I want very much to live near to them and visit them." The second was a clear, unemotional kind of reply such as "I take it for granted," or "it seems natural to me." Only in the third kind of positive reply does an outspoken emotional component come through: this idea "gives me a feeling of security and happiness" or "it makes me feel calm and peaceful."

One might expect that the negative replies would be more clearly tinged with emotion. Yet again three different shades of feeling are clearly discernible. The first is factual: "I have no such intention." In the second kind of reply, the emotional element comes through quite clearly: "this idea does not make me happy" or "it frustrates me." The third type of the negative reply is so agitated and full of hatred that its tone sounds strange in the atmosphere of parent-child relations we have described. Here are some examples: "the idea makes me shudder," "it shocks me," and "it nauseates me." Unfortunately, there is no way of establishing whether these are the comments of deeply disturbed adolescents, as one might imagine.

Table 5-11

The Idea of Living at the Same Place as My Parents . . .
(Percent)

	Boys (n = 155)	Girls (n = 173)
Affirmative reply	58.3	50.3
Negative reply	10.4	13.9
Undecided reply	31.3	35.8

As far as the "undecided" reply to the problem of living at the same place is concerned, our qualitative examination brought out a new aspect of parent-child relations, one we had not intentionally included in our questionnaire. We frequently met a replay that did not deal with the nature of relations to parents, but which reflected a view of parents as agents of socialization on behalf of the kibbutz, both in a positive and in a negative sense. The interrelation between the attitude of the adolescent to his parents on the one hand and to the kibbutz on the other is a complex one. One frequently finds a direct transition from the question about living with the parents to a reply concerned with living in the Kibbutz. Needless to say, this interaction between relations to parents and to the kibbutz may have a manifold content. It is quite obvious that a passionately negative relation to parents may drive the youngster out of the kibbutz. On the other hand, it is understood that strong, positive relations to parents forge a strong link with the kibbutz.

Yet the interrelation we are dealing with is more complex than that. We found replies which showed that the parents were clearly identified with the kibbutz, so much so that feelings for the parents merged and became one with feelings for the kibbutz. For instance, [this idea] "exists for me, because I love the kibbutz"or "It does not disturb me, as I want to live in the kibbutz" or "it makes me want to stay in the kibbutz, everything for the sake of kibbutz." We also found this reciprocal relation negated: "it is not relevant for me; it is not because of them that I'll stay in the kibbutz or leave it."

Parents in the kibbutz thus represent both a home and a set of values. We saw above that social ideals get a relatively low ranking in the system of values of kibbutz adolescents. In the replies we are dealing with just now, we have further proof of the adolescent's conception of the kibbutz as home. The aspect of shared values is not mentioned here at all; the adolescents use a specific term when they indicate their intention of living on a kibbutz. Invariably they use the Hebrew equivalent of the English "to dwell," which in itself puts the emphasis on the *home* and not on the ideological identification with their parents' value system. In short, parents in the kibbutz in their role as socializing agents are more successful in implanting in their children a feeling of being at home than in conveying to them the social values of the kibbutz. Outside observers are often so impressed by the difference between the social regime in the kibbutz and that of their own society that they tend to make hasty generaliations. In particular, there is a tendency to confuse equality in material possessions with uniformity in taste and to expect that similar standards of living result in similar interests and needs. Differences in taste and interests exist among individuals and among individual members of the same family within the kibbutz work, as in the world outside.

In our research, we asked questions aimed at investigating whether congruity of interests exists between kibbutz parents and children. We asked about the choice of work and pastime, about preferences for a particular branch of art or of science, about involvement in political affairs, and about the choice of a hobby. The number of responses to the long series of questions on this subject was high. Of the abundance of data given by the computer, there were very few findings which attested to homogeneity of interests among parents and offspring. We took into account only those replies where at least one-third of the youngsters indicated interest similar to that of one or both of their parents. The result which emerged is quite astonishing. The highest similarity we found was in the inclination to spend free time alone, a result which quite clearly expresses the kind of atmosphere in the home. We were rather surprised to discover that the next highest trait, a trait common to parents and offspring, was a lack of interest in science and politics (concerning girls, the lack of interest in science, shared with both parents, was even higher than that of boys). The highest positive measure of congruence we found was in the shared interest of boys and their fathers in agriculture. In all, the similarity among parents and their adolescent children, comparatively speaking, was highest in the area of work. There were also a few findings which suggested a similarity of interest in music.

There cannot be any doubt that the few findings which show homogeneity of interests are far from proving decisive parental influence in this area; they are a minute proportion among a wealth of results which disprove any such influence. Kibbutz conditions in no way cramp the growth of individual tastes and interests.

Influence of Age, Sex, Familism

So far, we have considered our sample of adolescents as a unit and have investigated the division of influence between parents and peers and the nature of parent-child relations. We shall now turn to the third main topic of our research, the variations which resulted when we applied three variables to our material—the age of the adolescent, the sex, and the influence of familistic orientation. We wanted to see if age played any part in influencing opinions and attitudes at two different stage of adolescence, at the ages of 14 and 17. With girls, we found that the only differences are in the sphere of personal relations, in matters dealing with friendship and love. Here, there was more friction among the older girls and their mothers although the girls credited their mothers with influence on their ideas and decisions. This finding reinforces a conclusion we drew earlier: at adolescence, ambivalence in relations to parents is an indication of their existential importance. With boys the differences between the two age groups are more conspicuous; with them, feelings of ease in the company of the peer group grows significantly with age. A complementary result emerged from our investigation into sources of friction: friction with other boys on status in the group is greater with the younger group. With the younger group, too, the influence of both parents was found to be more significant in matters pertaining to love and friendship while the influence of the father was greater in political matters and the influence of the mother was greater on the approach to matters of principle.

Two conclusions may therefore be drawn. First, the main impact of age lies in a changing division of influence between parents and peers: the influence of peers becomes weightier in various areas at the later stage of adolescence. Yet this increasing influence of the peer group appears only with boys. The variation which shows up in girls as they grow older lies in their more positive relation to their mother, not to their peer group. The last result is consistent with our other findings which concerned the differences in attitudes between boys and girls. The most striking has been the difference in approach to the group, a difference which was most clear-cut in the groups of the youth communities of Kibbutz Artzi where the group is at its most comprehensive; here it is not restricted to school hours, but comprises most of the social activities as well. In all four sections of our sample, girls felt more than boys that the peer group demanded a great deal from them, with girls from Kibbutz Artzi being 17 percent above the average of all four sample sections. This fact may well account for a greater sense of strain felt by girls of all four sections in their group life. The most telling fact in this respect is that girls feel much less ($p = .001$) at ease with their group than boys. We also found that in political and kibbutz matters girls are much less involved with the peer group than boys. In view of all these observations, it would appear that girls benefit less from life in a peer group than boys.

Another significant fact concerning sex differences emerges from our material: the main pattern of influence is oriented on the same sex, in both parent-child and peer relations. This pattern manifested itself very clearly in the various spheres of influence which we investigated:[j] school matters, love and friendship, matters of principle,[k] and the adolescents' personal future. In our investigation of causes of friction the same pattern appeared, only in reversed form.

The third variable to be investigated in our sample was the effect of *private* as opposed to communal *sleeping arrangements*. As we said before, when the child reaches adolescence, sharing of the parents' apartment is discontinued. What concerns us here is the influence on certain adolescents of a stronger familism which they experienced at a younger age. Three main differences clearly emerged from our material.

(1) There were indications that in the kibbutzim with a familistic orientation the influence of the parent of the opposite sex was seen to be greater than in the three other sectors: girls had a greater sense of ease in the company of their father and were more influenced by him in school matters while the mother played a greater role in discussions on the boys' future. In other words,

---

[j]The level of statistical significance was .01 or .001.

[k]In political matters the paternal influence was found strongest in both boys and girls.

as far as the attraction to the parent of the opposite sex is concerned, the structure of the family here seems to tend more to the traditional.

(2) We noted earlier that in our sample taken as a whole, there was very little similarity of interests, of choice of work, etc., between parents and children. The picture is somewhat different in the section of our sample from kibbutzim with familistic tendencies between parents and children. Here, similarity in the mode of spending free time is significantly higher than in the three other sections of our sample; the same is true of similarity in interests between father and son, for instance, in the choice of a hobby and even more so (p = .01) in artistic activity.[1] On the other hand, in the sphere of political influence, the fathers' influence on the daughters was significantly higher (p = .01) in the three sections where familistic tendencies do not prevail.

(3) The influence of the group was found to be consistently lower in the family-oriented section of the sample than in the other three sections, even though contact with the peer group is not weaker than in two other sections of the sample who study at district day schools, as opposed to the all-embracing youth communities of Kibbutz Artzi. This was illustrated in many ways. The feeling of ease within the group of peers is seen to be significantly stronger where common sleeping arrangements prevail. Friction within the peer group about life-style was most frequent among girls raised in kibbutzim with private sleeping arrangements. In school matters, girls in kibbutzim with common sleeping arrangements had a stronger influence on the other girls than did their counterparts who grew up in kibbutzim with private quarters. There was only one case where boys raised in kibbutzim with communal sleeping arrangements were more critical of the group than their peers in the other section, namely, in the assertion that they had to spend too much time with their group. This sort of criticism would not be heard among members of a group raised in a family-oriented kibbutz.

We see, then, that there are variations in the section of our sample raised in kibbutzim with a familistic orientation. These variations are both specific and univocal. However, one should not forget that the variations concern only part of our findings. At present, they constitute a variation inside the general social and educational structure of the kibbutz. Yet it may well be that in the future these divergencies in outlook may grow and lead to a distortion of the values and the way of life which are characteristic of the kibbutz.

The findings of our research confirm the importance of the peer group in the sphere of love and friendship, an area of major existential importance in the life of adolescents. We have compared the group in the youth communities of Kibbutz Artzi with the peer group in Kibbutz Meuchad and Ichud, i.e., with

---

[1]Whereas in certain cases congruity of interests in a family may benefit the child, enriching his cultural life by the acquisition of his parents' culture and taste, in other cases it could mean cultural deprivation or a desire for social isolation.

youngsters who study at district schools during the day and return in the early afternoon to their home kibbutz. The peculiar atmosphere of a closely knit group, living in an environment catering only for youth, manifested itself in the lack of friction over life-style for both boys and girls. With boys (not girls) the influence of the peers in problems of love and friendship was stronger here than in any other section of our sample. Other indications of the intensity of group life in this youth community are the high frequency of conflicts in the peer group on school matters and interpersonal problems arising in the peer group, as well as in the heated discussions within the peer group on political and general kibbutz matters, with girls in the main playing the role of objects for the influence exerted by boys. In two other spheres, the findings here were not different from those in the other two sections: the pattern of influence remained primarily among members of the same sex while the position of girls in the group was in general weaker.

Parents' Views

The last part of our research concerned itself with the differences in views expressed by parents as compared with those of their adolescent children. In our sample 388 parents (207 mothers and 181 fathers) of the 330 adolescents replied to the questionnaire. The parents' questionnaire was shorter, and it dealt with the following areas: appreciation of the time spent together with their adolescent children; feelings of ease in the company of parents and peers; causes of friction, spheres of influence, and the readiness of the parents to take educational initiative. All the questions were formulated in a manner corresponding to those given to the adolescents on the influence of parents and peers. The differences in appraisals made by parents and by adolescents can be summarized under four headings.

Appraisal of Parent-Child Relations

The parents in our sample ranked their own impact higher than their sons and daughters did.[m] This was the case in the following areas: feelings of ease of the adolescents in the company of their parents, politics, friendship and love, the approach to matters of principle, and the personal future of their children. Parents also ranked their own readiness to take the initiative in educational matters higher than their adolescent children did. There was only one exception to this rule: both boys and girls ranked the father's (but not the mother's!) initiative in matters of education higher than both parents did.

---

[m] All the results reported are statistically significant, more than two-thirds of them on an .001 level.

Evaluation of the Peer Group

The parents' responses show greater appreciation for the influence of the peer group than their childrens' responses. They ascribe to the group a greater influence on the political opinions of their children than do the adolescents themselves. The same overestimation of peer influence is revealed in matters concerning love and plans for the future. At the same time, parents also assume that the group causes more frictions than the adolescents testify to, both in the evasion of practical obligations and in matters of love and friendship.

The Adolescents' Appraisals of Fathers and Mothers

With the exception of the adolescents' assessment of the fathers' willingness to take the initiative in educational matters to which we have just referred, the parents' own assessment of the mother's role and the mother's assessment of her influence on the formation of political opinions were both higher than the assessment of their adolescent children. The only aspect of the mother's role quoted as a source of contention was the pressure she exerted toward the choice of a particular occupation. In general, the most conspicuous feature of the results is that adolescents value the role of the mother less highly than she does herself.

Causes of Friction and Differences in Their Assessment

In our comments thus far, we have noted that parents assess both their own influence and the influence of the group on the adolescent higher than their children do. In only three causes of friction were adolescents higher in their assessment than their parents: political opinion (with parents), school matters (with both parents and peers), and matters of life-style (with peers). Our results show that the gap between the self-conception of the mother and the evaluation of her role by the adolescent child is especially wide. This is not surprising if we take into account the problematic condition of women in the kibbutz and the need of the woman to reassure herself of her status. Similarly, parents' overemphasis on the value of the parental role may be an expression of parental narcissism which induces them to take such a stand in order to assert themselves in an environment with a dual-centered educational system. Our second finding, however, is surprising and demands some attempt at interpretation. We see that parents assess the influence of the peer group as greater than their children do and that they assess some of the sources of friction in the group lower than their children do. There may be two interconnected explanations. Parents may wish to show their loyalty toward the other main agent in the upbringing of their children, and they may wish to demonstrate their loyalty to their own past as members of a youth movement (personal communication from Professor S. Nagler).

We find a number of interesting modifications when we introduce the three independent variables we used in our research—namely, age, sex differences, and the differences between children raised in private as opposed to communal sleeping quarters—to our investigation of the differences between parental and adolescent assessment of influence. The difference in replies given by 14- and 17-year-olds is particularly instructive. We find that parental influence is greater with the younger age group while friction with parents is more frequent with the older age group. In the investigation of our second variable, i.e., the difference of sex on opinions and attitudes, we found 29 significant differences in evaluation between fathers and mothers, and of these 27 confirm that the pattern of influence in our sample is same-sex-oriented: in most of the areas investigated, we found that fathers believe they have greater influence on their sons than they have, while mothers claim greater influence on their daughters than their daughters attest to. An exception to this rule appeared in only one of the four sections of our sample—the section where there are private sleeping arrangements.

One question immediately presents itself here. Has the close proximity between parent and child in kibbutzim with private sleeping arrangements created a closer acquaintance of parents with their children so that differences in assessments of their relations are less common than in kibbutzim with communal sleeping arrangements? Our findings have not shown anything of this kind. This is not surprising when we consider that in most parts of the world parents and children live in close proximity but the physical closeness does not result in greater mutual understanding during adolescence.

One might assume that parents whose young children sleep in their apartments would see more of their adolescent children than parents in the three other sections. If this were so, we would not expect parents in familistic section to be partners to the complaint that they have too little time to spend with their children, as voiced by parents in the other sections. In fact, parents in both sections put forward this complaint with equal strength. It seems, then, that this complain has its roots in some psychological need of the parents which is not affected by organizational changes. Nor was our other expectation fulfilled: in both the sections which are compared here, parents assessed their own capacity to take the intiative in educational matters higher than their youngsters did. In short, in our material, we did not find any confirmation of the assumption that parents in the familistic section understand their children better. When we compared the assessment of relations made by parents in the communal and in the familistic sections of our sample, two main differences became evident. In the familistic section, the influence of the parent of the opposite sex was assumed to be greater, both on the personal future of the adolescent and in the sphere of friendship and love. The second difference appeared in the parents' appraisal of the causes for friction: the evasion of practical duties in the family home of the familistic section achieved a much greater weight than in the communal section. It seems then that private sleeping arrangements bring back to the kibbutz family many of the problems characteristic of the conventional family.

Thus our results cast light on many aspects of parent-peer-adolescent relations in the kibbutz. The most relevant result is the important role kibbutz parents play during adolescence. The general picture which emerges is of an interrelationship unique in its character and positive in its influence on the growing personality.

There are three factors which together have enabled the growth of this unique relationship. The first is the social structure of the kibbutz which has put an end to economic dependence of the child on his parents. The second is the child-centered attitude reigning in the kibbutz; child-centeredness is based here not only on the love each parent feels for his child, but also on an additional factor which lends it strength in the community as a whole, the fact that children represent continuity for this voluntary community. The third factor is the form of the dual-centered educational system: its very structure ensures that parents are not ever-present, that they cannot be taken for granted to the degree which, in family education, frequently gives the adolescent a feeling of "too much of a good thing," thus stimulating him to look for a peer group which is unconnected with the family orbit. In the kibbutz, even at adolescence, parental presence is eagerly sought. As we have seen, in the kibbutz reality, we are dealing with another *kind* of relationship, different in nature. Such a relationship makes it possible for the adolescent to reach his central goal—psychological autonomy—with less effort, both because he has no need to rebel against economic dependence and because from early childhood onward he is familiar with two worlds, both emotionally meaningful. In addition, peer relations are not acquired in adolescence at the expense of emotional ties with the parents; they exist from early childhood.

We do not believe that all the elements which together forge the new quality of parent-child relations are exclusively bound up with the specific conditions of kibbutz life. Urie Bronfenbrenner and his colleagues have repeatedly called attention to the advantages which cooperation between two socializing agents engenders. A child who has been brought up by a single socializing agent is likely to become more dependent on him, while a child raised by multiple agents learns that his security is not likely to be jeopardized.[26] In other words, Bronfenbrenner argues that a pluralistic as opposed to a monistic system of socialization has great advantages in the raising of an autonomous individual. And, indeed, if we compare the cardinal elements of kibbutz upbringing with other forms of social life and child socialization, we see that kibbutz experience has much to offer.

References

1. Howard Halpern, "Alienation from Parenthood in the Kibbutz and America," *Marriage and Family Living*, February 1962.

2. Bruno Bettelheim, *The Children of the Dream* (London: Macmillan, 1969).

3. Margaret Mead, "Some Theoretical Considerations on the Problem of Mother-Child Separation," *American Journal of Orthopsychiatry* 24 (1954): 477.

4. J. Hole and E. Levine, *Rebirth of Feminism* (New York: Quadrangle Books, 1971), p. 306.

5. A.I. Rabin, *Growing Up in the Kibbutz* (New York: Springer, 1965).

6. Menachem Gerson, "Parents' Tasks in Communal Education," in *Collective Education of Small Children* (Tel Aviv: Sifriat Poalim, 1947). H.

7. Ludwig Liegle, *The Family's Role in Soviet Education* (New York: Springer Publishing, 1975).

8. E.G. Devereux, R. Shouval, Urie Bronfenbrenner, et al., "Socialization Practices of Parents, Teachers and Peers in Israel: The Kibbutz versus the City," in *Child Development*, June 1974.

9. A. Shapira and M.C. Madsen, "Cooperative and Competitive Behavior of Kibbutz and Urban Children in Israel," in *Child Development*, 1969.

10. M. Kaffman, "Family Conflict in the Psychopathology of the Kibbutz Child," in *Family Process*, 1972, p. 171.

11. S. Nagler, "Clinical Observations on Kibbutz Children," *Israel Annals of Psychiatry* 1, no. 2 (1963).

12. M. Smilanski and Sarah Smilanski, "The Intellectual Development of Kibbutz-Born Children of 'Oriental' (Middle Eastern and North African) Origin," preliminary draft (Jerusalem: The Henrietta Szold Institute, 1968).

13. E.E. Maccoby and S. Feldman, *Mother Attachment and Stranger Reactions in the Third Year of Life*, Monograph of the Society for Research in Child Development, no. 37 (Chicago: University of Chicago Press, 1972).

14. The children's community of Mishmar HaEmek has been described at its early stages by: Edwin Samuel, *The Children's Community of HaShomer HaTsair at Mishmar HaEmek*, Mishmar HaEmek, 1943 (out of print). For a later, comprehensive description of its achievements and problems, cf. Bertha Chasan, ed. *From Generation to Generation* (Tel Aviv: Sifriat Poalim, 1948). H.

15. M. Alon, "The Educational Group at Adolescence," in his recent book *Youth in the Kibbutz* (Tel Aviv: Sifriat Poalim, 1975). H.

16. B. Bettelheim, *The Children of the Dream*.

17. Urie Bronfenbrenner, Ron Shouval, and Sophie Kav-Venaki, "Anomalous Reactions to Social Pressure of Israeli and Soviet Children Raised in Family vs. Collective Settings," *Journal of Personality and Social Psychology* 32, no. 3 (1975).

18. Michael Nathan and Aliza Schnabel, "Changes in the Attitudes of Kibbutz-Born Adolescents toward Going Steady and Sexual Relations," in *Studies on Education* (School of Education, Haifa University, 1975). H.

19. Rabin, *Growing Up in the Kibbutz*.

20. M. Gerson, "Kibbutz Parents and Their Adolescent Daughters," in *Essays on Kibbutz Education* (Tel Aviv: Sifriat Poalim, 1968). H.

21. Cf. Martin Gold and Elisabeth Douvan, eds. *Adolescent Development* (Boston: Allyn and Bacon, Readings in Research and Theory, 1969).

22. D.P. Ausubel, *Theory and Problems of Adolescent Development* (New York: Grune and Stratton, 1954).

23. F.J. Coleman, *The Adolescent Society* (New York: Free Press of Glencoe, 1961), pp. 311–313.

24. E.Q. Cambell, "Adolescent Socialization," in D.A. Goslin, ed., *Handbook of Socialization: Theory and Research* (Chicago: Rand McNally, 1971).

25. Ausubel, pp. 225–226.

26. R. Shouval, S. Kav-Venaki, and Urie Bronfenbrenner, "Anomalous Reactions to Social Pressure of Israeli and Soviet Children Raised in Family versus Collective Settings," *Journal of Personality and Social Psychology* 32 (1975): 480. Cf. also Bronfenbrenner, *Two Worlds of Childhood* (New York: Russel Sage Foundation, 1970).

6   Caregivers

Day care has become in modern society an urgent and widespread need and so have the problems of caregivers,[a] their approach to the children in their care, and their cooperation with the children's parents. In the kibbutz the caregiver is one of the earliest socializing influences in the life of the young child. Together with the parents she is responsible for the care of the child until the age of 3 or 4, when the child proceeds first to nursery school and then to regular primary school. At these later stages, the teacher becomes the dominant influence, while the *metapelet*, the caregiver, is relegated more or less to the status of a house-mother, providing the child with certain services, but no longer being an active mentor. Many caregivers working with school children resent this limitation. But for any broadening of their task they are dependent on the goodwill of the teacher, which is not always forthcoming. In this situation it is not amazing that Bronfenbrenner has found in his study of 12-year-old kibbutz children[1] that in this age group, the *metapelet* is no rival of the mother for the child's affection and that in their relationship to children, discipline and punishment play a much greater role than in the relations to the children of both parents and teachers.

When we speak of the *metapelet*, we do not refer to a baby-minder who provides a kind of day care service in order to free the mother for other tasks. We speak of a responsible worker in a system of education which functions according to shared educational principles and with specific educational aims in mind. The system carries within it the potential for rivalries and tensions which demands close cooperation between parents and caregivers if it is to succeed and, if investigated, can yield valuable insight into human motives and problems within a kibbutz setting. An exploration of these aspects of kibbutz dual-centered upbringing as they pertain to the *metapelet* working with toddlers will be our main concern in this chapter. We chose this particular age group because it is only for this limited period of time that the work attitude of the *metapelet* as educator can be assessed. In both the pre- and posttoddler stages she plays a secondary role, either to the mother or to the teacher.

There are two fundamentally different approaches to early childhood education. The Soviet approach wants to shape the individual according to the needs of the new Soviet society, even at the expense of personal spontaneousness. A

I wish to express my gratitude to Frida Katz (Kibbutz Gat) who advised me on this chapter, drawing on her rich experience in this field.

[a]Hebrew: singular: *metapelet*; plural: *metaplot*.

Soviet manual for preschool education appeared in Russia in 1962,[2] and its requirements were made obligatory throughout Soviet Russia. The manual aims at achieving early proficiency in language, in motor development, and in the acquisition of Soviet norms of morality. Group play at as early an age as possible is encouraged to promote the early growth of collective consciousness. In contrast to this rigid system of personality shaping, in the Western world from infancy onward emphasis is placed on the cultivation of individual initiative and on the encouragement of an individual pace of development. This approach has been expressed, for instance, by Susan Isaacs.[3] According to her, the child should be regarded as an individual whose feelings should be taken seriously: adults should encourage him to experience his environment actively by allowing him to run and jump, to build and paint. The child should be encouraged to play in a group and to develop his capacity for self-assertion and individual achievement.

The kibbutz movement as a whole has adopted the approach formulated by Isaacs. The unauthoritarian social structure of the kibbutz could not tolerate an educational approach directed toward the demands of a centralistic, authoritarian social regime. As an innovative and progressive body, the kibbutz in general and the educational committees in particular have always been open to influence and have changed their approach to keep pace with the progress of educational theory. At first, in early child care in the kibbutz framework the main emphasis was on early sex education and the importance of friendly relations with both parents and caregivers. Now, in accordance with recent psychological thought, additional emphasis has been placed in early childhood education on the orientation of the child in his physical and social environment. Thus, the caregiver who is encouraging the child's curiosity by answering his innumerable questions is considered to play an active part in the development of the child's emotional stability and ego strength.

Day care institutions which employ caregivers are found in many countries. But there are three features which are specific to the *metapelet* in the kibbutz. First, when the child reaches the age of 18 months, all duties involving child care are carried out by the *metapelet*. Thus the parental tie with the child has mainly an emotional character. This kind of clear division of tasks could hardly exist in a regular day care center. Second, the ties which bind parents and caregiver are close and manifold. Even if a *metapelet* is inclined to adopt a posture of professional distance, she cannot possibly do so. She herself is a member of the same kibbutz as the parents with whom she works. Frequently, she is known to the parents from her childhood days. The same system of social values holds for both parents and *metapelet*: more often than not, the *metapelet* herself has children and members of the kibbutz can easily find out whether, as a mother, she does what, as a caregiver, she preaches. The social situation in the kibbutz neither allows the *metapelet* to assume the role of a professional authority, remote from parental criticism, nor compels her to be obedient to clients on whom she depends for her livelihood. In this situation, cooperation between equals becomes the only positive solution possible. Third, the ratio of *metaplot* to children is exceptionally high in the kibbutz: it is even higher than the ratio of one caregiver to five toddlers as accepted in Denmark.[4] In Ichud and Kibbutz Meuchad we find one permanent *metapelet* for four children while in Kibbutz Artzi there are two permanent *metaplot* for six. In most cases, some additional help is given by nonprofessionals. Cooking and laundry are dealt with by the central services of the kibbutz. The time schedule which is set up allows the *metapelet* to give maximum attention to the individual child and enables her to participate in informal play periods of children, even if such periods are not scheduled for the whole group.

Although from the early days of kibbutz living it was taken for granted that a teacher needed full professional training, those responsible for early child care were considered able to do their work well with a minimum of training. It took years of persuasion until in 1961 a study course of one year was started at Oranim, the School of Education of the kibbutz movement and another ten years until the course was extended to two years. But not all kibbutzim or all kibbutz federations utilize the facilities offered at Oranim to the same degree.[b]

A long and full period of training is not only important as a means of increasing professional knowledge and, consequently, professional competence. It also serves an important purpose in raising the social status of the caregiver to that of a professional. We believe that the introduction of professional training as an obligatory requirement for all caregivers in the kibbutz would serve three important purposes: it would safeguard educational standards; it would give a greater degree of permanency among caregivers in the kibbutz;[c] it would increase the opportunities for professional work open to women.

Kibbutz educationalists have always believed that a dual-centered upbringing confers great psychological benefit on the child. Where the child is dependent exclusively on the ability of the mother to care for him, where he is at the mercy of her preferences, where her intense emotional involvement may influence her judgment, his developmental needs may not always be the primary consideration in his upbringing. Nor is it common for a mother, particularly in the Western world, to admit her misgivings and seek professional guidance. With all this in mind, kibbutz educationalists have assumed that habit training, social learning, and autonomous behavior could be encouraged greatly by a professional caregiver who is less emotionally involved with the child than his mother. This assumption has become one of the tenets of the kibbutz upbringing.

---

[b]This is a further expression of the differences among individual kibbutzim to which we have referred several times. In any given kibbutz, the amount of training required of its caregivers is an indication of the importance accorded by the members to education.

[c]In 46 percent of the toddler groups we studied, the caregiver was changed at least once.

Whereas in other communities the caregiver is regarded as a necessary substitute for the working mother, in the kibbutz the *metapelet* is regarded as a complement to the parents.

Research on Metaplot

It was with a view to testing these accepted assumptions that in 1970 the author and his team[d] conducted research on the *metapelet* in early child care in the kibbutz.

The research focused on two main topics: the behavior of the caregiver in her role of educator with a toddler group and her attitude, as declared by her, toward both the children in her care and their parents. A third topic which we tried to include did not produce clear results. We attempted to determine the *result* of different forms of *metapelet* behavior by measuring the degree of autonomous behavior achieved by the children in her care.

The behavior of the *metapelet* was measured through time-sampled observation, her attitudes through an attitude scale. Since we were concerned with *metaplot* working on their own, we chose the age group of toddlers (from 1½ to 4 years) for our investigation of *metapelet* behavior. We wanted to get an overall picture of all the activities in toddler groups; we therefore chose a representative random sample of the three kibbutz federation. We came up with a weighted random sample of 106 caregivers. The most laborious part of our teamwork was devoted to the unequivocal definition of the behavior categories to be used in our observation. We are greatly indebted to C.E. Moustakas[5] and his associates who devised and clearly defined almost all the observation categories we have used (see Table 6-2).

Initially we thought that our behavior categories should be divided into three headings of evaluation: positive, negative, and neutral behavior. According to our philosophy of child rearing, we felt we could safely interpret encouraging the child's activity as a positive mode of *metapelet* behavior and physical punishment as a negative one. We were inclined to classify a category like "directing the child" as a *neutral* behavior category. The unequivocal language of statistically significant correlations taught us that it made no sense to hold on to the assumption that there are "neutral" modes of behavior. If a behavior category proved to be correlated significantly and exclusively with negative behavior categories, we had to evaluate this category itself as a negative one. In order not to burden our text unduly with statistics, we want to quote here only one example

[d] I am much indebted to Rachel Danon, Lotte Ramot, and especially to Aliza Schnabel, who also took care of the statistical analysis and the tabulation of our results. I also wish to express my gratitude to Dr. Charles Greenbaum of Hebrew University who was our advisor on methodology and statistics. His knowledge and personal interest greatly benefited our research.

in detail. It concerns the category of "directing the child" which we had regarded as a neutral one, but which was shown to be clearly negative. See Table
6-1.

A similar surprise, though this time resulting in a positive behavior category,
occurred concerning the category "restricting the child while offering alternative
or explanation."[6] Theoretically we had also classified it as a neutral behavior
category, but its correlations made it clear beyond doubt that it belongs to the
positive behavior categories. We would like to note that we introduced the observation category "*metapelet* seeking praise" because both Spiro and Irvine[7] as-
serted that this sort of behavior of *metaplot* was a frequent occurrence in kibbutz upbringing. They interpreted it as an attempt of the caregivers to allay their
own doubts and feelings of insecurity about communal education. We reached
therefore the conclusion that we needed to group our material under two headings only: positive and negative behavior of the *metapelet*. Table 6-2 summarizes our results. The percentages mentioned denote the frequency of a certain behavior pattern during the period of observation of our sample. See also
Table 6-3.

Let us now try and spell out the meaning of the facts and figures we have
reported so far. What answer do they give to the fundamental question about the
educational content of the work the caregiver performs?

The first salient fact evolving from our findings is that negative modes of
metapelet behavior amount to only 21.32 percent while in our representative
sample positive behavior forms amount to 78.68 percent. In evaluating this result, we have to take into account that we are dealing with *metaplot* of toddlers,
an age group which is difficult to handle. It is worth noting that among the nega-

Table 6-1

Behavior Categories which Have Significant Correlations with Directing

Behavior	r
Giving permission	.19[a]
Limiting use of objects	.42[b]
Deprivation of affection	.18[a]
Ignoring	.19[a]
Corporal punishment	.26[b]
Threatening	.49[b]
Criticism of child's person	.25[b]
Physical restraint	.50[b]
Forbidding	.42[b]
Promising reward	.24[b]
Criticism of child's action	.43[b]
Frustrating the child's activity	.32[b]

[a]$p = .05$.
[b]$p = .01$.

Table 6-2

Twenty-two Categories of *Metapelet* Behavior

	n = 106		
	Mean	Standard Deviation	Percentage
Recognition of the child	50.90	19.70	12.67
Joint participation in activity	18.30	10.40	4.53
Giving reassurance	30.80	11.10	7.70
Giving affection	19.40	11.80	4.73
Physical help	51.80	14.30	13.00
Orienting, offering information	84.60	33.40	20.54
Giving permission to proposed activity	9.30	9.40	2.17
Encouragement of activity or achievement	39.50	22.20	9.38
Restricting by offering alternative or explanation	15.95	7.06	3.96
Total of positive behavior categories	320.55		78.68
Combination of seven infrequent negative behavior categories	7.32		1.88
Threatening	5.39	6.10	1.34
Physical restraint	3.89	5.38	0.97
Forbidding	8.51	6.69	2.13
Directing	37.39	16.00	9.38
Promising reward	3.96	4.88	0.95
Criticism of child's action or production	18.93	10.80	4.67
Total of negative behavior categories	85.39		21.32

For the sake of perspicuity we have combined in Table 6-2 seven negative behavior categories whose frequency was very low. We deem it necessary to indicate the content of the seven behavior categories included.

Table 6-3

Seven Infrequent Negative Behavior Categories

	Mean	Standard Deviation	Percentage	n[a]
Limiting use of objects	2.70	2.60	0.7	77
Frustrating the child's activity	0.96	1.89	0.24	35
Metapelet seeking praise or physical affection from the child	0.67	1.74	0.18	23[b]
Deprivation of affection	0.10	0.36	0.03	9
Corporal punishment	0.42	1.39	0.11	13
Criticism of the child's person	1.56	2.25	0.39	52
Ignoring the child	0.91	2.50	0.23	27
Percentage of total *metapelet* behavior			1.88	

[a]This column indicates the number of *metaplot* observed in whom the behavior denoted did appear.

[b]When compared with the assertions of Spiro and Irvine, this column allows for two interpretations: either their casual impressions were not justified even at the time in which the authors worked, or communal education in the kibbutz has changed very much indeed.

tive modes of behavior, there is only a negligible amount of the worst methods of child rearing, such as corporal punishment, deprivation of affection, etc.

Our findings show that the kibbutz child grows up in an atmosphere of affaction and reassurance and that careful attention is paid by the caregiver to his behavior and growth, even at a time when she makes no active contact with him. Our observations showed a constant and conscious attempt to give the child as much information and support as possible in order to help him to become familiar with all the aspects of his physical and social environment.

Two other modes of caregiver behavior are closely interrelated with this attempt: encouragement of the child's activity and restriction of the child's activity while offering alternative activity or, at least, explanation. It would be naive to assume that the inexperienced small child could be allowed to do whatever he likes; if only for the sake of avoiding the harm he might inflict on himself or on other children, sometimes his activities have to be restricted. But the manner in which the restriction is carried out is of great importance. Forbidding or frustrating his activity may make him feel that there are mysterious dangers hidden in the environment and that therefore he has to learn to restrain his wish to explore reality. But restriction by explanation, followed by a proposal of an alternative activity, will not arouse this tendency to shy away from reality. On the contrary, it will help the child to familiarize himself with his environment and thus strengthen his ability to trust people and feel confident in the world around him. One other difference should be clarified here—that between orienting and directing. *Orienting* sets the stage for the child's own activity; he is allowed to use his own initiative. *Directing* imposes on him a defined activity or duty which may not be in keeping with his interests or his capacity. It may not be possible to bring up small children without ever directing them. But the recourse to directing will be less frequent if a thoughtful educator becomes aware of its true psychological meaning.

One more remark is in order about those 17 caregivers in our sample of 106 who were shown to be "seeking praise or affection from the child." The figures involved are small, and the importance of correlations should not be overrated. Still, we want to mention the modes of behavior significantly correlated with it: these include giving affection to the child, criticizing his personality, and, the highest correlation, using physical punishment. Without going deeper into the personality problems of such a caregiver, the image of the caregiver which emerges from these facts is that of an insecure adult who tries to allay her fears through emotional dependence on the child in her care.

There were some variables which had influence on *metapelet* behavior.[e] The standard of equipment of the nursery had an influence on *metaplet* behavior, amounting to 2 percent: the better the equipment, the higher the positive behavior. The age of the children in our sample made for certain differences in *metapelet* behavior: it was at its lowest with the youngest children (1.6 to 2.6), at its

---

[e]They were not sampled for in our research design in the same way as those so far mentioned.

highest with the middle age group (2 to 3), and declined again when the children approached the nursery school age (3.5 to 4). Yet all these variations were small. The predominant impression arising from this research is one of an amazing similarity in the behavior of the *metaplot* observed.

The greatest variation in caregiver was found when *metaplot* belonging to different kibbutz federations were compared. In Kibbutz Artzi, the number of caregivers whose behavior was evaluated as positive was shown to be 1.4 percent above the average of the whole sample; in Ichud, they reached the overall average while in Kibbutz Meuchad they were almost 2 percent below the average. The variation here amounted to 3.6 percent. The differences among the three federations in this respect, nevertheless, remain quite narrow. The dominant impression of the *metapelet*-child relationship in the three kibbutz federations is the similarity among them, a similarity which is reflected in each case by the high achievement[f] in the educational behavior of the caregivers. We should not lose sight of the fact that we are speaking of a group of paraprofessionals who work with a particularly difficult age group.

The high achievement of kibbutz *metaplot* seems to be a result of the special conditions which exist in the kibbutz community. The *metapelet* deals with far fewer children than her counterpart in town. She works with children of the kibbutz to which she herself belongs; she understands and accepts the demanding educational standards set by the kibbutz; she wants her own children to enjoy the same treatment as she dispenses to the children in her care; she knows that the educational climate she creates in her group influences her own standing in the community.

The life of the kibbutz *metapelet*, however, is not easy. She has no opportunity to create the sort of professional distance enjoyed by her colleague in a day care center. Her greater involvement with the children makes for greater demands on her emotional resources. She is aware of the fact that in a small community, it will be hard for her to rid herself of the stigma of failure should she be unsuccessful in her task.[g]

We had expected that some of the psychological difficulties experienced by the caregivers would be exposed when they were asked about their attitude to children. After all, it is much easier to make high-sounding declarations about one's attitude to child care than to apply them in actual practice. Thus we expected the replies of *metaplot* in our attitude scale to be much more self-flattering than the marks we gave on observed behavior. Yet, whatever the social pressures might have been, they did not appear in the replies. Caregivers did not succumb to the temptation of making statements according to the demands of

---

[f]When asked to compare our results with the mode of rearing the small child in middle-class United States, two American professors of psychology gave widely divergent replies.

[g]The insight into this feature of communal life has sometimes led young enthusiasts who founded a kibbutz into a crisis of disillusionment.

social desirability. On the contrary, there was an astonishing likeness between observed behavior and attitude statements. Applying the educational philosophy described above, we classified the *contents* of an attitude statement as positive or negative. We found that 79.3 percent expressed a positive attitude to children, 16.4 percent a negative attitude, and 4.3 percent could not make up their minds on a specific attitude statement. When we compare this average with the average of observed positive behavior—78.68 percent—the similarity is striking. See Table 6-4.

What is the educational significance of these replies? We should bear in mind that the respondents are young, not trained properly, and that children at the toddler age are most difficult to work with. Yet the replies given reveal that these young *metaplot* have a clear and definite approach to their work. They reject a merely custodial approach (22)[h] which in fact absolves the *metapelet* from her educational responsibility toward the child. They do not belittle the queries of the small child (23), nor do they regard the caregiver's authority as the sole basis for educational success (10). They reject the temptation to make the toddler emotionally overdependent on his caregiver (15), nor do they try to influence him or win his affection by offering him rewards (7). Instead, they guide the small child and express their own affection for him with good humor and active encouragement (28) (33). Since their approach is child-oriented (20) (25), they insist on individualization when dealing with his needs (3) (26). The practical difficulties inherent in this approach are indicated by the considerable number of minorities which appear in some of the replies (17) (30). That these replies cannot be regarded simply as pious declarations of socially desirable behavior is shown once again by the astonishing similarity between the results obtained in the questionnaire and those obtained from direct observation.

Cooperation between Parents and Caregivers

Close cooperation between parents and caregivers is an essential feature in the theory of communal education. Let us see now how it functions in day-to-day practice. Theoretically, caregivers and parents play complementary roles: the parents fulfill the emotional needs of the growing child while the *metaplot* meet his instrumental and achievement needs. But this theory[8] of a clear division of duties which developed when the instrumental functions of parents were greatly restricted is certainly not applicable under present conditions. The *metapelet* may demand more of the child than his mother does because the *metapelet* spends more time with him and carries a greater share of his orientation toward his group. For his part, the child may respond to the atmosphere of affection

---

[h]The figures in parentheses denote the number of the statement in the attitude scale.

Table 6-4
Attitudes toward Children

Statement	Percentage[a] Agree	Percentage Disagree	Percentage Undecided
3 We are not in the army where everything has to work according to schedule.	89.7	10.3	
5 Small children cannot appreciate the caregiver's effort.	26.4	64.2	9.4
7 A child should be rewarded for proper behavior.	14.1	81.1	4.8
8 A sense of humor is a very important tool in the caregiver's work.	88.7	6.6	4.7
10 Small children cannot play together without direction by the caregiver.	12.3	84.9	2.8
14 This modern freedom ruins the child!	7.5	90.6	1.9
15 I love work with small children because I may cuddle them as much as I wish.	12.1	82.1	5.2
17 One should not force a child to do something he does not like.	67.0	33.0	
18 What a pity our educational system leaves so little authority with the caregiver.	17.9	77.4	4.7
20 One should never interfere with children at play.	63.3	35.8	0.9
22 The first priority in the caregiver's work is to keep the house clean for the children.	5.7	93.4	0.9
23 It is not worthwhile to reply every time the child asks the stupid question of "What's that?"	16.0	80.2	3.8
25 Freedom of movement for young children prevents running away at a later age.	76.4	11.3	12.3
26 In a group one has to demand the same from every child.	7.5	92.5	
28 A smiling face and an encouraging word are the best recipe for a child's sorrow.	83.2	15.0	1.8
30 A child should be made to understand at a very early age that the toys in the children's house are not his alone.	66.0	31.2	2.8
33 A friendly smile achieves more than a loud shout.	83.1	13.2	3.7

[a]n = 106 caregivers.

and reassurance which the *metapelet* creates by offering her expressions of warmth and emotion.

When these role distinctions become blurred, a potential source of conflict arises. It is easy to see the reasons for such conflict in the parent-caregiver relationship. Unlike her counterpart in town, the kibbutz mother has to cooperate with another adult from the earliest days of her child's life. She leaves her child in the care of the *metapelet* through the night with all a mother's attendant concern about his welfare. One might expect the mother to try to rationalize her sense of uneasiness and discontent by finding fault with the *metapelet*. Any inclination toward criticism on the part of the parents would thus seem "natural." Both mother and *metapelet* may have conflicting expectations concerning their roles and the forms of behavior which should be permitted or prohibited. Just as the mother may feel a sense of conflict over the proper division of her time between the child and her other responsibilities, so the *metapelet* may experience similar inner stresses over the best apportionment of her time among children in her group, their parents, and her own family.

In different periods of kibbutz development, different potential sources of caregiver-parent conflict have prevailed. In the earliest days of kibbutz living, when the *metapelet* had to work ten hours a day with no prospect of formal training, when hygienic conditions were very primitive, tensions were often felt, by both tired *metaplot* and strained mothers.

But even in the ordered conditions which have prevailed in kibbutzim for the last thirty years, conflicts may arise, often internal conflicts of the parents which are projected onto the *metaplot* and the children's house. A common example is that of parents who are considering leaving the kibbutz and who use the children's house as the focus for their general discontent. There are also parents who do not accept the cooperative values of the kibbutz and bring up their child to be competitive and aggressive. Another potential source of conflict is the greater heterogeneity of today's kibbutz population. Newcomers to the kibbutz may come from the U.S., from Oriental countries, from a city or a moshav in Israel. Difficulties caused by different tradition of mother behavior are greatest as far as Oriental Jews are concerned, where even such habits as nursing or weaning a child may be different. It is no easy task for a young *metapelet* to cope with the problems arising from this heterogeneity.

There are, of course, also psychological factors which bring about conflict situations between parents and caregivers. In this book we do not deal with psychohygienic problems. But we want at least to mention some pathogenic factors. Our views derive from and are in accord with those of Nagler.[9] In kibbutz conditions a negative attitude of parents toward the children's house as such or toward a particular *metapelet* have a strong pathogenic impact on the child. The structure of kibbutz upbringing does not allow the caregiver to keep a professional distance, and therefore one's own feelings of failure and guilt are easily projected on the other socializing agent. The fears of mothers, stemming from their own personal history, are easily transferred to the children's house. Such is the case also concerning internal strife in a family. Nagler has related a detailed case history which illustrated how easily the dark hours of night, with the child "alone" and far away from his parents, lend themselves to this sort of projection.

Let us see now how frequent these potential tensions between parents and caregivers of small children are. In 1962 Rabin[10] interviewed 123 young kibbutz mothers (81 of them kibbutz-born), mostly mothers of infants or toddlers. Nearly all the mothers said that their children were happy in the children's house and that both parents and children were satisfied with the arrangement. Concerning their relations with *metaplot*, between 80 and 90 percent indicated rather positive attitudes toward the *metapelet*, even though 59 percent expressed the opinion that she was not ideal. Only 4 percent related that they often opposed the opinion and practices of the *metaplot*. These findings are quite astonishing, in view of the potential for conflicts we described above. In his important paper on family conflict in the kibbutz,[11] Kaffman compares parent-child interaction in a group of 192 emotionally disturbed children with a control group of 124 children 3 to 18 years old. In the group of emotionally disturbed children, a lack of consistency between parents and educators and conflicting approaches and relations were recorded in 15 percent of the disturbed children; in the control group these conflicts amounted only to 7 percent. This finding confirms that conflict situations between parents and educators are infrequent. It also confirms Nagler's observation that neurotic parents quite often find relief in their own personal problems by criticizing communal upbringing.

Just as changes constantly occur in other spheres of kibbutz life, so relations between parents and caregivers also alter in different periods. In Rabin's research, many mothers complained that they did not have enough time to spend with their small child. To alleviate the burden of their complaint, during the last twelve years work arrangements have been modified in order to enable mothers to meet their young children during the morning as well. The most important among these changes is a new orientation in the guidance of *metaplot*. While at first the work of the *metapelet* was exclusively child-centered, more recently her links with the *parents* of her group have been given greater significance. But bringing about a change in attitude is a laborious and time-consuming process which must be given its main impetus by careful training. This implies an additional focus in the program which now has to include not only child psychology, hygiene, play techniques, etc., but a sound course in human relations and sensitivity training. I believe that in this respect the best results so far have been achieved in the training of infant nurses.

Our research on *metaplot* working with toddlers also dealt with the problem of *metapelet* and parents. There were fourteen attitude statements in our attitude scale dealing with relations between *metaplot* and parents. They were focused on two main problems:

1. The attitude of our 106 *metaplot* toward cooperation with parents (Table 6-5)
2. Their opinions concerning the division of influence between parents and caregivers on the child's development (Table 6-6)

We may summarize our findings as follows:

(1.) There is overwhelming support for close cooperation between parents and *metaplot*. Three of the accepted statements (6) (21) (34) clearly contradict the assumption that *metaplot* and parents regard one another as competitors for the child's affection. Another highly supported statement (24) asserts the positive emotional effect on the *metapelet* of strong ties with parents of her group.

(2) In spite of this basic approach, the division of opinion about allowing visits from parents at *any* time of the day (11) indicates that there is a practical problem inherent in the principle of open house: parents may disrupt an

Table 6-5
Attitudes toward Cooperation with Parents

Statement	Percentage[a] Agree	Percentage Disagree	Percentage Undecided
2 Close contact with parents spoils the caregiver's judgment.	20.8	79.2	
4 Parents may visit in my group only at fixed hours.	14.2	85.8	
6 A child's happiness makes the parents content with his *metapelet*.	88.6	3.8	7.6
11 Visits of parents at any time they wish strengthen their ties with the *metapelet*.	57.6	37.7	4.7
16 Always listen to parents' advice.	98.2	1.8	
19 Parents evaluate a *metapelet* according to the cleanliness of the children's house.	6.6	91.5	1.9
21 As the *metapelet* succeeds, the mother becomes increasingly jealous.	12.2	84.0	3.8
24 Strong ties with the parents of my group are a great boost for me.	95.3	2.9	1.8
32 Mothers are happy when the *metapelet* succeeds.	98.1	1.0	0.9

[a]$n = 106$ *metaplot*.

Table 6-6
Opinions on the Influence of Parents and *Metaplot*

Statement	Percentage[a] Agree	Percentage Disagree	Percentage Undecided
9 A mother's feelings are always the best guide for the understanding of the child.	52.8	45.3	1.9
13 The children's house is capable of guiding the child in the right direction.	84.0	12.3	3.7
27 The *metapelet* knows what is good for the child, not his emotional mother.	10.4	83.9	5.7
29 A child is a duplicate of his parents, and there is nothing a *metapelet* can do about it.	7.6	88.6	3.8
34 It is the objective judgment of the *metapelet* which leads her to the understanding of a child.	88.7	6.6	4.7

[a]$n = 106$ *metaplot*

activity of the children by their visit. In other words, any monopolizing approach of parents to their children is rejected.

(3) An overwhelming majority reject the notion that parents conceive of the role of the *metapelet* merely as housekeeper, and not as educator of their child (19).

(4) *Metaplot* are fully aware of the unique emotional ties which connect the child with his parents (16). Therefore they reject an approach which refuses to grant the "emotional mother" competence to decide what is good for her child (27). But as soon as this negation of the mother's competence is omitted, in a similar statement (34) they strongly support the importance of the objective approach of the *metapelet* which leads her toward understanding of the child.

(5) When the *metaplot* express their opinion in *principle* about the influence of parents and children's house in the life of the child, they strongly reject the notion that a child is a mere duplicate of his parents and emphasize that the children's house has the power to influence and mold a child's development (13) (29).

Thus, our research leads us to conclude that in the great majority of cases the relationship between parents and caregivers is one of harmony, not conflict.

We mentioned in Chapter 2 that the small size of toddler groups and the high ratio of caregivers have contributed greatly to the success of communal upbringing. We have now to add here that they have also created one of the greatest problems which the kibbutz has to face. The form and size of the groups and the number of caregivers were determined at a time when family size in the kibbutz was small (an average of 1.5 to 2.0 children). Since then, the average family size has grown, reaching 2.8 at present. The demands of the children's house on the workforce resources of the kibbutz are, therefore, a constant problem in kibbutz planning. In general, the dynamic character of the kibbutz economy and its rejection of hired labor together create a perpetual workforce shortage. The question of whether the kibbutz economy can support the present ratio of adults to children has once again been raised. In the situation as it exists today in most kibbutzim, some modification in the present rate of adult work-hours or in the ratio of *metaplot* to children must be made. It will not be easy to persuade members to overcome the resistance to the change that such a modification will entail since both *metaplot* and parents are used to the present ratio of caregivers to children.

One suggested solution to the problem of providing adequate child care without too great a drain on kibbutz resources is that put forward by advocates of familistic trends. But they do not realize that the solution they propose runs counter to the *social* aspect of the problem. The familistic "solution" would, of course, put an end to any attempt to broaden the occupational opportunities for women in the kibbutz.

A recent survey by Raanan Sas[12] has substantiated the adverse effects of changes in kibbutz upbringing which have resulted from the growth of familistic tendencies: mothers no longer accept the division of tasks between mother and caregiver as previously prescribed. They demand a greater degree of participation in child care and greater authority in decisions which concern their own children. If this new attitude to the *metapelet* becomes widespread, her work is likely to become subsidiary to that of the mother. Although most of the *metaplot* enjoy work with children and feel that their work is less routine than a service job in the kitchen or the laundry, one can still hear two complaints: they dislike working in the evening hours, and mothers frequently do not accept their authority as professionals.

There is an internal contradiction between the first and the second claim: *metaplot* cannot expect to get professional status as long as in their own scale of values the overriding consideration is a familial one with job involvement coming second. The one-sided emphasis on family life deprives these *metaplot* of the opportunities kibbutz life can offer them, namely, a synthesis of motherhood and meaningful work. A solution to these problems can only be achieved by the women themselves, acting in solidarity.

References

1. Cf. E.C. Devereus, R. Shouval, U. Bronfenbrenner et al., "Socialization Practices of Parents, Teachers and Peers in Israel," *Child Development*, no. 45, 1974.

2. Henry Chauncey (ed.) *Soviet Pre-School Education* (New York: Holt, Rinehart and Winston, 1969).

3. Susan Isaacs, *Childhood and After* (New York: International Universities Press, 1949), pp. 62-65.

4. Cf. M.G. Wagner and M.M. Wagner, "Day Care Programs in Denmark and Czechoslavakia," in E.H. Grotberg, ed., *Day Care: Resources for Decision* (Office of Economic Opportunities, 1971).

5. Clark E. Moustakas, Sigel, and Schalock, "An Objective Method for the Measurement and Analysis of Child-Adult Interaction," *Child Development* 27, no. 2 (1956).

6. We would have been less surprised had we known Reinhard and Anne-Marie Tausch's lucid evaluation of guiding and directing teacher behavior. Reinhard Tausch and Anne-Marie Tausch, *Erziehungs Psychologie* (Gottingen: Verlag fur Psychologie, Hogreve, 1971).

7. Melford E. Spiro, *Children of the Kibbutz* (Cambridge, Mass.: Harvard University Press, 1958), p. 30. Elisabeth Irvine, "Observations on Kibbutz Education," *Human Relations*, 1959.

8. It was put forward by Rivka Bar-Joseph, "Patterns of Socialization in the Kibbutz," *Megamot* 11, no. 1 (1960), Jerusalem. H.

9. S. Nagler, "Clinical Observations on Kibbutz Children," *The Israel Annals of Psychiatry* 1, no. 2 (1963), Jerusalem.

10. A.I. Rabin, "Maternal Attitudes to Kibbutz Child Rearing," *American Journal of Orthopsychiatry* 29 (1964).

11. M. Kaffman, "Family Conflict in the Psychopathology of the Kibbutz Child," *Family Process* 11 (1972): 171-188.

12. R. Sas, "Division of Tasks between Parents and Educators in Early Child Care in the Kibbutz," thesis, 1973. H.

7 Epilogue

The Second Kibbutz Generation

Even though we shall use the all-inclusive term *second kibbutz generation*, it should be borne in mind that we are not speaking of a homogeneous group.[1] Differences in talent and temperament, in interests and aspirations, are found in the kibbutz as in the world outside. Nor does the term refer to one age group: in the older kibbutzim, many youngsters now approaching maturity belong to the third kibbutz generation. The most distinctive feature which unites all members of the second kibbutz generation and separates them from the founders is that they were born into the kibbutz way of life. This simple statement may seem so obvious as to be superfluous. Yet it is from this fact that so many other differences among the generations derive. Unlike the founder generation, who chose the kibbutz way of life from among many other possibilities, who saw in the kibbutz an ideal to be pursued even in the most adverse circumstances, the second generation takes the kibbutz for granted. For kibbutz children in their early years and later as youngsters and then as adults, the kibbutz is primarily a home. They do not see it mainly as a task group, idealistically carrying a national and social message. They accept without question the parents' home and the children's house. As their world widens, so they take for granted the landscape, the peer group, their work and life-style.

Yet the system of social values which prevails in the kibbutz does not come "naturally"—it has to be acquired. Whereas the original group of founders was gradually formed through a long and arduous period of selection, the second kibbutz generation was automatically accepted as belonging to the group. For the second generation, the acquisition of physical dexterity and a capacity for endurance is not an aim in itself, as it was for their fathers: they are used to it since early childhood. Nor have they known at first hand the struggle to realize the Zionist longing for the ingathering of Jews from the Diaspora. The search for a national home, the social and physical challenges and struggles, the hard-won achievements of the founder generation are no longer a part of the lives of their children.

But the changing circumstances have created problems for the second kibbutz generations which their parents did not have. Denied the kind of opportunities for self-fulfillment which were the lot of the founders, their children need to look for satisfaction in other ways. There is now a growing interest in work which demands expertise. This desire for specialization and job satisfaction

121

is met by the needs of the kibbutz which have introduced industrialization and the mechanization of agriculture. Whereas the founder generation was prone to indulge in ideological discussions in a constant attempt to clarify and define the aims of kibbutz life and of human existence in general, the younger generation is interested primarily in practical ways of ensuring personal satisfaction for each individual. This does not imply that they are superficial. The number of people with an ideological or philosophical interest may be relatively smaller in their ranks; but I believe that there are among them comparatively more people who are artistically creative or technically gifted.

Apart from the personal achievement obtained in specialized work, in cultural activity, or in creative work within the kibbutz, there are two other ways in which members of the second generation can achieve a sense of self-fulfillment. The first is through service in the army. In their dedication to military service, a cardinal national requirement blends successfully with personal needs: the army gains many able, dedicated soldiers while the individual finds an opportunity to develop his potential and to widen his experiences by meeting people from all strata of Israeli society.

The second way in which kibbutz-born youth can achieve a greater measure of self-realization is by leaving the kibbutz for a year. The most usual time is the postarmy period. The transition from his previous role as an officer to his new one as a regular worker in the kibbutz is not an easy one. Previously he often had to make important decisions; in his new position he may sometimes feel that his potential is not fully utilized. Thus he asks for a year's vacation in which he earns his own living and, more often than not, enough money to finance a period of travel abroad. This is an innovation and the result of a hard fight by the kibbutz-born youngsters against a frequent attitude of older members who saw in the suggestion an unwarranted extravagance. After the October War in 1973, the demand for such a year off became more pressing. Experience has shown that the great majority of these young people return to the kibbutz after comparing dissimilar ways of life, making a conscious choice. It has become clear that in leaving their home for a while, the young people do so not because they reject kibbutz values, but because they want to look at these values in a more detached way. There is, however, one most unfortunate fact we have to mention. While the course described has become an almost regular pattern for young men in the kibbutz, there are very few young women who demand such an interim period. It is more difficult for women to earn a lot of money in a short time; it is also more difficult for them to be on their own in the world. Needless to say, the absence of exciting experiences for the women creates another obstacle in the attempt to change the traditional image of women in the kibbutz. It may be one of the factors which make family life so important for women of the second kibbutz generation.

Nowadays young people in many countries sense an animosity against all-embracing ideologies as well as against orthodoxy and closed-mindedness—and the kibbutz born generation is no exception. They know that social values cannot be inherited from the previous generation. Members of the young kibbutz generation have never experienced victory of socialist ideals. What they have witnessed in their lifetime was the unmasking of Stalin by the Twentieth Communist Congress; they met Russian weaponry in Sinai, weaponry intended for the destruction of the Jewish state; they learned of anti-Semitism and labor camps in Soviet Russia. Yet the kibbutz is run on Socialist principles and has always fostered its affinities and connections with the great socialist movements and parties outside Israel. Kibbutz youth found, therefore, that either they had to share the perplexity which is nowadays the lot of so many socialists in so many countries or they tended to deprive socialism of its political content and regard the kibbutz as the only true and legitimate form of socialism. In both cases, Zionism has come to take precedence over socialism in their system of ideological values, the emotional identification of kibbutz-born members with Israel as their homeland and with Zionism as the pillar of their belief system. There have, of course, always been some who grasped the depth and complexity of the conflict between Israel and its Arab neighbors. In the aftermath of the 1973 war, this understanding has comprised much broader circles. Certainly, this is the issue which has made many members of the second generation painfully aware of the vital importance of an ideological and political problem.

The "psychological moratorium" described by Ericson as characteristic of modern adolescents is found with unique strength among kibbutz youth. In many ways, this moratorium comes to an end when kibbutz youngsters enter the army. Although they have an inclination to cling together, circumstances force them apart and into a meeting with the various strata of Israeli society with which they have had little previous contact. Now they meet the social problem cases, the high school dropouts, and members of the "other" Israel. They are made aware of the different sources of status, of the high status accorded to the army officer, the state official, and the university professor. They hear of the career-oriented attitude of urban schools and parents, and they see the effect of the social gap between Jews from Western and those from Eastern backgrounds. The effect on kibbutz youth of this confrontation with the world outside is powerful. It reveals itself in different ways. For some members, it forces a confrontation with kibbutz values which results in greater social activity on their return to the kibbutz; for others, it creates an urge to realize their intellectual abilities or artistic potential and results in a desire to delay a return to regular work in the kibbutz. Still others are driven into the privatism Kenneth Keniston has described.[2] They increasingly emphasize those areas of life which are least involved in the wider society; on return to the kibbutz they display a stout consumer orientation, frequently combined with strong familistic tendencies.[a] Still,

---

[a]As we have seen above, this orientation has got numerous followers in the founder generation as well.

people who are inclined to associate the kibbutz with a country club should not overlook its work regime: 3½ free days per month, two weeks of vacation during the year, a visit abroad once or at the most twice in a lifetime.

The older members of the second generation have found scope for their activity inside the kibbutz mainly in the economic sphere, and those who seek public activity have found it in army service. Women of the same group make their main contribution in education and the service branches. In the younger age groups of this generation, cultural activities and study play a much greater part. In both age groups, one area of activity, politics, has been largely omitted from the range of their public activities. The ideological disappointments mentioned above may provide one explanation for this fact. It is also true that the various socialist parties in Israel have only recently begun to rejuvenate the ranks of their leadership.

There is another factor which has shaped the attitudes and activities of the second kibbutz generation in a decisive manner. War, to many of the members of this group, has become a constant threat and a recurring reality. Many of them have fought in three, and some even in four, wars. The threat of war has created one of those "critical situations" which are instrumental in shaping the image of a whole generation. Kibbutz youngsters excel in fighting, but they loathe warfare. The true attitude to war of members of the young kibbutz generation is revealed in a wonderfully human document, *The Seventh Day*,[3] a collection of impressions and emotions gathered in conversation with kibbutz soldiers after a surprisingly short war and overwhelming victory in 1967.

Two themes run like a thread through these interviews. The first is deep concern for humanity, expressed both in words and in recorded action. In reading the conversations it becomes clear that it is no easy matter to have to live through successive wars and still to remain a sensitive, feeling human being. The participants in this conversation express a foreboding that their war experience may change their human image, may make them cynics or Arab haters. N. Raz, a teacher as well as a political leader, has voiced his deep concern about cheapening life. Yet Raz was also forced to draw a realistic conclusion, a conclusion which seems hard for progressive intellectuals far removed from the dangers confronting Israel to grasp: right without might is meaningless.

By now, ten years later, the impact of war and regular military service in the reserve has remained a weighty factor in shaping the attitude of the young kibbutz generation[b] (as indeed for the young generation in Israel as a whole).

How does the experience of battle influence kibbutz youth today? In order to stand the strain, they have to shut out the sensitiveness for human suffering which their upbringing has deeply ingrained in them. Does this hardening con-

---

[b]Here I can draw on some personal conversations with young officers in my own kibbutz. They cannot be regarded as a representative sample, only as an illustration of the influence warfare has on young leaders, important for the future development of the kibbutz.

tinue in civilian life, too? Does it create a cynical attitude toward human values and a permanent change in the behavior patterns which are essential for life in a kibbutz? High-sounding talk without practical implication is certainly despised by them. There is also a need to find release from the terrible strain battle imposes on men, especially if the fight was long, as it was during the War of Attrition. Men had to find relaxation, by resting, in sexual encounter, even in getting drunk. However, it is my firm impression that these reactions are of a temporary nature. The best among these products of a happy and secure childhood were transformed by their battle experience into adults who are keen to lead a life full of activity and dedication to the kibbutz, as opposed to privatism and a mere consumer orientation. The demanding and strictly regulated framework of army service leaves them with a desire for independence and responsibility. Their meeting with the problems of leadership, with the needs of the wounded and the suffering of bereaved families whom they visit, gives them a heightened understanding of human relations. Quite often, the shared experience of regular service in the same unit, sometimes under battle conditions, creates ties which are as strong as or even stronger than those which bind the individual to the peer group and leads to a better understanding of a different way of life and of value system.

My partners in conversation spoke to me also about the profound emotional experience of facing death on the battlefield. One of them referred to it as a gamble with life. Sabras do not often speak of their feelings, especially when asked to remember a time in which there seemed little hope of survival. Those who did speak of it related that they did not think primarily of ways to survive. They carried out their duties responsibly, even when seriously wounded. If they thought of civilian life in this predicament, they thought of a festive occasion in the kibbutz or of their sweetheart. One said that he could easily understand people who in this situation were turning to religion. This way was not open to him, he added, because Israel's religious establishment was exploiting religious feelings politically.

Thus, it appears that for the type of people we have described the experience of warfare has mainly had a temporary effect. The hardships of war did not turn them into cynics. Their capacity for forming human relations as well as their wish to contribute actively to life in their kibbutz seem to have deepened under the impact of war.

The Seventh Day was written by a group of young kibbutz members with Abraham Shapira as principal editor. The penetrating conversations held with soldiers created a strong bond among the participants. Later on, this affinity of attitude found its expression in a quarterly, *Ssedemot*, initiated by Ichud. It has now become the mouthpiece of an interfederational group of young kibbutz members. They are a group whose members share an orientation to philosophical as well as to kibbutz matters and, more recently, also to political issues. From the quantitative point of view, they are a minority in their own generation. But their sincerity, courage, and desire to tackle questions of principle have made them important spokesmen of their generation. When, in 1967, they witnessed the liberation of Jerusalem, a deep sense of national continuity came over them. It was not interest in archeology such as now interests so many Israelis. It was a sense of continuity with a spiritual heritage, a concern about its significance for the present. Quite a few members of the *Ssedemot* group are in search of metaphysical meaning in life. Yet these religious leanings have not obscured the boundary which separates them from orthodox groups in Israel.

The desire for sincerity and the objection to cant has made many members of the young kibbutz generation impatient of patriotic cliches. In their opinion, an attempt to educate youth toward identification with the state of Israel, as such, without heading its character and quality is an education toward fallacious generalities.[4] It is consistent with this attitude that the *Ssedemot* people have a basic quarrel with members of Gush Emunim,[5] the fanatic orthodox group. Their meeting proved that there was no common ground between the two sides in the discussion. On the one hand, there is an irrational orthodox approach which recognizes only the authority of the rabbi of the group and has a total disregard for political reality and democratic decision making and a contemptuous negation of Arab rights, all on the grounds that the whole land of Israel was promised to Abraham by God. On the other hand, we have a realistic view of Zionism, based on the realities of Jewish suffering and persecution in the Diaspora, a fundamental belief that Arab life and rights are equal to Jewish life and rights, a rational approach to national politics which cannot allow theocratic visions to prevail over democratic decisions.

Until the foundation of the state of Israel, the great majority of the Jewish population regarded the kibbutz as the realization par excellence of Zionist and socialist ideals. Though remote from the centers of political decision making, the kibbutz had no reason to feel isolated. With the foundation of the state, however, Ben-Gurion accused the kibbutz movement of neglecting the cardinal task— absorption of the new mass immigration. In the kibbutzim, his attack only strengthened seclusive trends which existed even in the founder generation, for it was quite a temptation to give preference to practical and constructive tasks over political involvement. Such inclinations, however, could not satisfy the majority of kibbutz members. They have regarded themselves as part and parcel of Israel's society and have understood the need for forging a living link with it. The recent political defeat of the labor movement has contributed to a greater political involvement of the younger kibbutz generation. They become aware of the growing social gap between Jews from Oriental and those from Western backgrounds, of the problem-ridden relations with the Arab community inside Israel, of the lowering of work ethics and morality in certain public and private spheres.

Still, when all is said and done, the political alertness of the young kibbutz generation seems wanting. Kibbutz youth have long since proved their ability to run the affairs of the kibbutz in all spheres. Many are also willing to perform a technical, military, or teaching job, even if it implies working outside the kibbutz. Yet there are comparatively few among them to tackle political tasks. What are the reasons for this astonishing attitude? One of them is probably the political disillustionment they have experienced. Another seems to be their view of the kibbutz as their home rather than a task group. Moreover, the kibbutz has reached a modest prosperity in the last decade. It is still a long way from the affluent society Galbraith has described[6] or even from the conspicuous consumption which today characterizes a large section of the Israeli upper class. Still, this economic standard makes it possible to stay on because of the economic benefits and security the kibbutz provides. The privatism of families of this sort does not blend well with political involvement. And the greatest danger which may befall a kibbutz is the oblivion of its socialist character and an appraisal of its achievements by capitalist criteria.

This problem has now been tackled in a significant area. For quite some time a few kibbutz high schools have tried to integrate Oriental children from their neighborhood into their school community. Kibbutz Artzi as a whole had previously not embraced this idea. In its large convention held recently, it has been decided to reverse educational policy: in all its high schools a considerable proportion of youngsters from Oriental origin will be integrated, both in order to serve a national need and for the education of the kibbutz children themselves. This decision was strongly urged by kibbutz youngsters of 17 and 18 who advocated it during the deliberations of the adult delegates. Does this suggest a turning of the tide?

A Necessary Change

We have no doubt that the kibbutz is here to stay. We have no doubt that it will continue to function as an exemplary community. We have no doubt that the members of the kibbutz will maintain a high work ethic, a high level of productivity, and will continue to live in a society in which the individual is free from dependence on coercive authorities and in which there is no crime. The questions which are worrying us are not those dealing with the mere existence of the kibbutz, but those concerned with its value orientation and possibilities for active involvement in Israeli life. We wonder whether a self-contained community would be able to give enough scope to its most creative, talented, and ambitious children. We wonder whether such a kibbutz would be able to attract the eager, original mind from outside; for if not, the kibbutz will shrink in stature and may eventually be forced to apply a rigid set of regulations in order to safeguard its very existence. This, in turn, would affect human relations within the kibbutz for the worse. We believe that the *quality* of kibbutz life is the crucial problem which the new kibbutz generation has to confront.

It is our considered opinion that the kibbutz must alter one of its structural tenets in response to the needs of a changing Israeli society. What we are suggesting is not a radical change, but an acceptance and extension of a move which began in the kibbutz some time ago.

When the first kibbutzim were founded, there were two cardinal tasks which faced the new immigrants: conquest of physical work by the Jewish town dwellers and cultivation of barren land. It was in accordance with these national needs that the kibbutz defined its tasks. The kibbutz was conceived as a living unit which contains both production and consumption. *Production* was defined as physical work to be done mainly inside the kibbutz. Even at this early period the spokesmen of the kibbutz upheld the socialist tenet that all kinds of work—physical and intellectual alike—should have equal value. But, in fact, preference was clearly and unilaterally bestowed on physical work, according to the actual tasks. Since then, the economy of both Israel as a whole and the kibbutz has become more diverse, as in every modern society.

Today many kibbutz members do not actually perform physical work. Their work is needed for administrative jobs, teaching, cultural enterprises, etc. This trend will continue: in 1975, 3160 kibbutz members continued studying after finishing high school, a figure which indicates the great alterations in the future workforce distribution in the kibbutz. Other kibbutz members began to work outside the framework of the kibbutzim, on behalf the the kibbutz federations, in higher education, in regional economic enterprises, in the army, etc. As we mentioned earlier, this movement toward specialization is not only a response to the diverse needs of the kibbutz but also a way of satisfying the need of the young generation for individual self-realization. So far these new developments are sometimes still controversial in kibbutzim; but I believe that in the near future they will be officially recognized. Such recognition will bring about a solution to two of the burning problems of the kibbutz. When membership in a kibbutz is not automatically identified with work inside the kibbutz, the ties of the kibbutz with Israel's society as a whole could be considerably strengthened. The danger of the kibbutz becoming a happy but isolated island in Israel's rapidly changing society could be averted.

Today every kibbutz is under obligation to put 5 percent of its members at the disposal of the kibbutz federation; most of these members take turns between work inside and outside the kibbutz, operating in many spheres of public life. If our suggestion is accepted, there will be more kibbutz members working on a professional basis as social workers, army officers, medical personnel, etc.—but they will remain active members of their respective kibbutz. In many cases, this might ease a situation of cognitive dissonance which increased the number of young kibbutz members who leave the kibbutz, even though they feel identified with its way of life. This change might also draw professionals who immigrated to Israel from the West to kibbutz life, people who feel strongly attracted to the social values the kibbutz embodies but are not prepared to abandon their professional work. Yet the most important prospect of such a modification in kibbutz life would be an increase in the influence of the kibbutz and in the penetration of *chalutzic* values into Israel's society. Throughout Israel, there would be people who would not regard personal status and an exalted standard of living as their main aim in life, but whose social allegiance makes them find their highest gratification in the service rendered to those sections of Israel's society which need it most.

We do not underestimate the problems and difficulties involved in such a change.[7] The greatest among them is being created daily by the dynamic character of the kibbutz economy which needs all workers available. This problem is so grave because a recourse to the employment of hired labor would automatically defeat its own purpose: it would damage the public image of the kibbutz as a socialist society which implements its values in real life.

The view we have put forward here entails a weighty alteration of the present conduct of the kibbutz. Yet this book has shown other changes which were effected in the kibbutz whenever developments in the kibbutz itself or changes in Israel's society necessitated. The capacity of the kibbutz to accomplish changes in its life testifies to its vitality. *Y. Chasan*, the veteran leader of Kibbutz Artzi, has superbly expressed this belief in the successful adaptation to change of the kibbutz movement in an address to his kibbutz, on the occasion of its fiftieth anniversary:[8]

I see before my eyes the community of youngsters . . . who laid the foundations for our kibbutz, 50 years ago. We still have maintained their capacity to dream. We are still able to feel what is imperfect in our life . . . and we are still drawn to the future. If I was granted the opportunity to return to our kibbutz as it was 50 years ago, nice and homely, or to live in our kibbutz as it is today, without hesitation I would choose our present life. What has been accomplished is more humane, more variegated and prolific than were all our dreams.

References

1. A comprehensive book by Menachem Rosner et al. on the second kibbutz generation has just appeared in Hebrew. Its English translation will soon be forthcoming: Menachem Rosner et al., *The Second Generation: Continuity and Change in the Kibbutz* (Tel Aviv: Tur Press).

2. Kenneth Keniston, "Social Change and Youth in America," in E.H. Ericson, ed., *Youth: Change and Challenge* (New York: Basic Books, 1963), p. 174.

3. Henry Near, ed., *The Seventh Day* (Penguin Books, 1971).

4. *Ssdemot*, no. 56 (1975): 42. H.

5. *Ssdemot*, no. 58 (1976). H.

6. J.K. Galbraith, *The Affluent Society* (London: Penguin Books, 1958).

7. M. Gerson, "Towards a Change in the Status of the Kibbutz," *Hedim* (the Kibbutz Artzi quarterly), no. (1972). H.

8. Y. Chasan, "To My Kibbutz on Its 50th Anniversary," *Al Hamishmar*, 27, no. 9 (1972). H.

Appendix
Martin Buber and the
Kibbutz Movement

In the 1920s and the early 1930s, the writings of Martin Buber had great influence on the Jewish youth movements of Europe. Buber's belief in the destiny of youth and his view of Jewish history as a struggle between official and hidden Judaism strongly appealed to youngsters who met Judaism mainly as a matter of three holy days. Buber's strongest personal involvement, though, was with the German-Jewish youth movement *Werkleute*.[1] Through an intensive and lengthy contact with Hermann (Menachem) Gerson, the leader of the *Werkleute*, Buber had a profound effect on the ideological and educational development of this movement.[2] In Buber's relations to the *Werkleute* two elements became increasingly prominent. One was Buber's emphasis on the importance of Jewish studies for the return of assimilated youth to Jewry and to Judaism; the second was Buber's growing understanding of the way in which small communities can influence society at large. This line of thought found its clear formulation in Buber's *Paths in Utopia* (first published in German in 1950). It is both a challenge to every form of coercive rule by a state apparatus and a statement of his anarchistic views. Here, Buber clarifies his profound belief in the historic role of small communities whose organization is based on self-rule.[3] On the basis of his wide and penetrating knowledge of the writings of Marx and Lenin, Buber formulates a thorough criticism of the Soviet Union. As it was voiced six years before the relevations of the Twentieth Party Congress on Stalin's crimes, his criticism was rejected by many left-wing intellectuals as a manifestation of utopianism, rooted in naive and wishful thinking and lacking insight into the tragic contradictions inherent in revolutionary change. This was also the approach adopted at the time by the two left-wing kibbutz federations.

If one reads his book today, one is immediately struck by Buber's historical insight. Buber makes two main points in his criticism of the Soviet Union's historical development. (1) He claims that orthodox belief in the prerogative of a party center, powerful in deciding doctrine as well as in dictating action, turns the theory of a "withering away" of state rule into mere wishful thinking. (2) He states that Bolshevism has deliberately blurred a distinction which is of vital importance, namely, that which should be made between ruling and managing the affairs of a society. Such a distinction is an absolute necessity in every form of life. Where it is not made, we have coercive rule of a self-perpetuating elite which has been the distinguishing mark of every dictatorship, in whatever form it found its expression, throughout human history.

In contrast to Soviet communism, Buber has defined his own concept of a genuine society. According to Buber, it cannot be a mere aggregate of unconnected individuals, because such a group could be held together by coercive rule only. The practical reconstruction of society can only be achieved by a change in the economic and political regime. Otherwise, the realization of socialism remains a lofty and remote ideal. But a mere change in the power structure does not create a new society. The true basis of a new society lies in the establishment of small communities in which members share a communal way of life and which are organized in federations. But such communities cannot fulfill their task when they remain isolated from their social environment.

One would have expected Buber to become a leading figure in the kibbutz movement, not only because of his personal contact with it but more so because the kibbutz (and moshav) have been the purest fulfillment of his social philosophy. He himself called them "an experiment which did not fail."[a] As a matter of fact, Buber's influence on the kibbutz movement has never been really great. Buber's philosophical and political views were quite unpopular in Israel from the 1930s to the 1960s, both within the kibbutz movement and in other influential groups. This was the period when two of the kibbutz federations consolidated their Marxist orientation and regarded the struggle for the establishment of a communist society in Soviet Russia as the central social event of the time. Buber's criticism and his emphasis on the need for social change achieved through small communities were regarded as the whims of an isolated intellectual who lacked the courage to embrace the great social revolution then taking place, because he was disturbed by the frustrations with which the Russian leaders of the revolution had to reconcile themselves in the service of the great cause. Buber's warning that there is no way which leads to an aim essentially different from itself was dismissed as the smug illusion of an intellectual who left the dirty work to others.

Nor were Buber's views on the need for Jewish-Arab understanding received any more warmly. While Buber became one of the leading advocates for such an approach,[b] the position of the Labor Party in Israel, under the leadership of Ben-Gurion, became increasingly intransigent.

Although there were two other areas in Israel where the kibbutz movement (and especially Kibbutz Artzi) could have regarded Buber as their authentic spokesman. On neither occasion was the opportunity exploited. One was in the crisis of the voluntary organizations after the establishment of the state of Israel. The adherents of the cult of the state denied the significance of voluntary groups once the state was established. This was contrary to Buber's anarchic approach, which led him to strongly oppose belief in an omnipotent state. In this, he regarded Ben-Gurion as his historical adversary. The second was in the opposition of the kibbutz movement to the entrenchment of the religious party in the government of Israel. Buber, too, was always a strong opponent of religious or-

---

[a]When I asked him once why he spoke of "exemplatory nonfailure" of the kibbutz rather than of success, his reply was, "Success in the realization of social ideas is a category suitable for the time of the Messiah."

[b]Buber's views on Israel's policy toward its Arab neighbors were similar to those of Kibbutz Artzi. In 1961 he told me that in all the *knesset* elections, he had cast his vote for Mapam.

thodoxy and especially of the combination of organized orthodoxy and government administration. One would, therefore, have expected the kibbutz movement to join forces with Buber. They did not do so, although the religious parties, aware of Buber's attitude toward their political aspirations, fought him bitterly at every opportunity and even tried, unsuccessfully, to withhold his nomi-
nation as honorary citizen of Jerusalem, though it was put forward in the very
last days of his life.

The question arises as to why the kibbutz movement did not regard Buber
as a valuable ally in those areas where their ideological positions converged. It
seems that the kibbutz movement did not welcome Buber into its ranks because
it was disturbed by the inconsistency between Buber's philosophy and the time
he chose for his immigration to Israel. Buber had been a Zionist from the time of
Herzl. But his immigration was delayed until 1938. The delay is explained in
the second volume of Buber's correspondence. In brief, there were his deep involvement in German culture, his hestitations about the transition to another
language, and his allegiance both to the great undertaking of translating the Bible
into German and to Franz Rosenzweig, his friend and coauthor. There was the
vital role he had to play in German Jewry after Hitler's rise to power. There was
also the vexing question of how far he could hope to find in Israel scope for active participation and influence.[4] All these reasons explain Buber's hesitancy, but
they do not remove the sense of uneasiness which the kibbutz movement felt
toward the man's practice of his own ideals.

A second personal inconsistency should be mentioned here. Even though
Buber's philosophy did not allow him to join a political party, he felt himself
very close in idea and spirit to the labor wing of the Zionist movement. In 1928,
he published a famous lecture on "Why the Upbuilding of Palestine Has to Be
Socialistic." Yet when he came to live in Israel, he did not regard the labor
movement (including the kibbutz movement) as the group with which he had
the greatest affinity. He preferred the academic world of the Hebrew University
as his reference group. Once in Israel, Buber adopted the role of a university professor and sought little contact with the kibbutz movement. There were, however, some exceptions. I vividly remember how pleased he was when, in the last
years of his life, he established personal contact with some young members of
the Ichud. And when a group of professors in Europe put funds at his disposal
for the planting of a forest in his name near Jerusalem, Buber decided to have
this memorial forest planted near Kibbutz Hazorea.

But on the whole, the dialogue between Buber and the kibbutz movement
never started in earnest. A great opportunity was missed.

References

1. Cf. Menachem Gerson, *Essays on Kibbutz Education* (Tel Aviv: Sifriat
Poalim, 1968). H.

2. This has been documented recently in M. Buber, *Briefwechsel Aus Sieben Jahrzehnten*, 3 vols., ed. Grete Schaeder (Heidelberg: Lambert Schneider, 1973 to 1975).

3. M. Buber, *Pfade in Utopia; Werke*, vol. 1 (Heidelberg: Lambert Schneider, 1962). First published in 1950.

4. Cf. the frank exchange of ideas on this problem between Buber and Gerson in *Briefwechsel*, vol. 2, Letters 486, 490, 492, 493.

Index

Index

Abraham, 126
Adolescence, 75–79; attitudes toward parents' in, 79–82; differences between parents' and children's views during, 99–102; education and, 23; freedom of contact with parents during, 71; modern research on, 82–87; personal relations during, 76–77; quality of relations in, 90–96, sex-role typing and, 42; sexual relations during, 78; spheres of influence in, 87–90
Age: acceptance of role of women and, 37; *metaplot* behavior and, 111–112; parent-child relationship and, 96–99, 101; survey on marriage stability and, 57–65
Agriculture, 14; adolescents' attitudes toward, 96; women's attitudes toward, 35–36
Aliyah: Second, 4; Third, 8, 21
Alon, M., 77
Arab countries, 12, 116
Army, 122
Asceticism, 15–17
Asphormass, Jehuda, 83
Austen, Jane, 29
Ausubel, 82, 85
Autonomy, 77, 102

Balfour declaration, 5
Bassewich, Lilia, 33
Ben-Gurion, David, 12, 132
Bernfeld, S., 21
Beth Alpha, 17; education and, 21; kibbutz federations and, 10; origin of kibbutz and, 5–6
Bettelheim, Bruno, 29–30, 46, 67, 77, 78
Birthrates, 46
Breast feeding, 71–72
Brenner, Givat, 83

Bronfenbrenner, Uri, 73, 77, 78, 102, 105
Buber, Martin, 6, 17, 131–134
Burgess, E.W., 45
Bussel, Chayuta, 20
Bussel, Joseph, 4, 19, 20

Campbell, 83
Canadian immigrants, 64
Capitalism, 53, 55
Caregivers, *See Metaplot*
Chalutzic values, 129; familistic tendencies and, 46, 56; immigration and, 12; kibbutz federations and, 9; origin of kibbutz and, 4, 7
Change, social, 38–42
Chasan, Yaakov, 10, 129
Child guidance clinics, 24
Childhood psychosis, 24
Children: divorce and care of, 70; economic dependence of, 55–56, 70–71; feelings of ease of, 85; men in rearing of, 39–40. *See also* Adolescence; Parent-child relationship
Children's house: attitudes toward work in, 35; identification in infant stage and, 22
Coleman, 83
Collective ego, 77
Collective ownership, 14–15
Collectivism, 4
Committees, 33, 34–35, 51
Communes, 45
Communism, 55
Concentration camps, 12
Conformity, 76–78
Consumer orientation, 53
Cultural factors, 2

Danon Rachel, 108
Day care, 105–107. *See also Metaplot*

De Beauvoir, Simone, 29
Degania: communal education and, 19–20; kibbutz federations and, 7; origin of kibbutzim and, 3–5, 6
Denial, 81
Denmark, 107
Deprivation, maternal, 68
Diaspora, 32, 121, 126
Directing behavior, 111
Discrimination against women, 32–33, 38, 39
Divorce: care of children after, 70; country of origin and, 62–65; duration of marriage and, 59; kibbutz-born and Israel-born persons compared for, 64; life for single person and, 60–61; for single person and, 60–61; remarriage after, 60–61, 62; survey on, 57–65

Eastern Europe, 46
Economic factors: differences between kibbutzim and, 2; divorce and, 59–60; familistic tendencies and, 54–56; family structure and, 48–49; gifts and, 54–55; parent-child relationship and, 102; principle of kibbutz living and, 3
Education, 19–25; attitudes toward women and, 36, 38; divorce and right to, 59, 60; dual-centered nature of, 102; in early kibbutzim, 68, 69; economic ties within families and, 54; father's influence in, 74, 99, 100; kibbutz family and, 49; parents' status in, 47–48, 98–99; remarriage and, 61; sex typing in, 40; social structure and, 21–23; in Soviet Russia, 105–106; structure of kibbutz and, 22, 23, 24; women's role and, 42
Ein Charod, 9
Ein Harod, 33
Elkind, 9

Engels, Friedrich, 27
Ericson, E.H., 123
Essenes, 4
European immigrants, 12, 21
Expressive sphere, 92

Family, 45–65; care of child and, 19; economic structures and, 48–49, 54–56; familistic tendencies of women and, 53–54; future of, 57–65; kibbutz family distinguished from other forms of, 48–57; kinship ties in, 54; non-kibbutz family compared with kibbutz family in, 58–60; role of women and, 37–38; sex typing and, 51–52; sleeping arrangements of children and, 50–54; social framework of, 49–50; stability of, 62, 64; task orientation of, 56–57
Fathers: adolescents' appraisal of, 100; education and, 49, 74, 99, 100; infants and, 72; influence of, 89, 99, 100; quality of relationship with, 90; role of, 74. See also Parent-child relationships
Federations, kibbutz: metaplot in, 112; organization of, 6, 7–11
Feldman, S., 74
Festivals, 61
Freud, Sigmund, 21, 22
Freudian school, 68, 69

Gain motives, 55
Galbraith, John Kenneth, 127
G'dud HaAvoda, 8
Germany, 54
Gerson, Hermann (Menachem), 131
Gifts, 54–55
Golan, S., 21
Golan, Yona, 33
Goode, W., 60
Gordonia, 7–8
Governing body of kibbutz, 2
Greenbaum, Charles, 108
Gronseth, Erick, 30

Guidance clinics, 24
Gush Emunim, 126

Hacohen, Eliezer, 17
Haifa, 59
Hakibbutz Hameuchad, 8–9
Halpern, Howard, 67
HaShomer Hatzair, 76; education and,
    21; kibbutz federations and, 10;
    origin of kibbutz and, 5–6;
    women's participation in, 34
Hechalutz, 32
Hever HaKvutzot, 8, 50
Hospitalism, 68
Housework, 41, 50

Ichud, 7–8, 125; communal moshavim
    in, 55; *metaplot* in, 107; peer
    group relations in, 98; sleeping
    arrangements for children in, 51,
    52, 53
Identification, 22
Ideological collectivism, 10
Immigration: changes in kibbutzim
    and, 12; conflict of values in,
    70, divorce and, 62–65; origin of
    kibbutzim and, 3–4; Second
    Aliyah, 4; Third Aliyah, 8, 21
Industry, 14
Infants, 22, 72–73
Isaacs, Susan, 106

Kaffman, M., 24, 74, 75, 116
Keniston, Kenneth, 123
Kibbutz Artzi, 129; adolescence in,
    75, 76, 77; attitudes toward
    women's work in, 35–36; educa-
    tion and, 23; kibbutz federations
    and, 10–11; *metaplot* in, 68, 69,
    112; parent-child relationships
    in, 46, 79–82, 84, 97, 98; sleep-
    ing arrangements for children in,
    53; women's participation in,
    33, 34
Kibbutz Meuchad: attitudes toward
    women's work in, 35–36; famil-
    istic tendencies in, 53; kibbutz

federations and, 9, 10, 11;
    marriage study in, 62; *metaplot*
    in, 107, 112; parent-child rela-
    tionships in, 79–82, participa-
    tion of women in, 33; peer
    group relations in, 98; political
    split in, 12; sleeping arrange-
    ments for children in, 51
Kinderheim Baumgarten, 21
Kinship ties, 54

Labor Brigade, 8
Labor Party, 10, 11, 132
Lenin, 131
Life-style, 100
Lifshitz, Michaela, 83
Locke, J., 45
Lubianiker, Pinchas, 7

Maccoby, E.E., 74
Madsen, M.C., 73
Managerial positions for women, 41,
    51
Mapai, 8
Mapam, 11
Marriage: acceptance into kibbutz and,
    13; acceptance of role of women
    and age of, 37; divorce rate and
    duration of, 59; in early settle-
    ments, 46–47; remarriage and,
    60–61, 62; sex-role typing and,
    29–30; survey on stability of,
    57–65; trial marriage and, 40;
    women's role in, 45
Marx, Karl, 131
Mead, Margaret, 67
Men: changes in attitudes toward
    women by, 41; sex typing and
    childrearing role of, 39–40; work
    attitudes of, 35–36
Messinger, Yehuda, 53
Metaplot: duties of, 74–75; in early
    kibbutzim, 68, 107; features of,
    106–107; importance attributed
    to, 21; during last months of
    pregnancy, 71; misconceptions
    of role of, 67; mother's relation-

ship with, 71–72; parents' co-operation with, 113–119; psychological benefits from, 107–108; research on, 108–113
Middle East countries, 64
Migration. *See* Immigration
Military service, 122–125
Mill, John Stuart, 28
Mishmar HaEmek, 75
Mortality rates, infant, 22
Mosharim, 4; attitudes toward parents by girls of, 79–80; child-rearing in, 68; education in, 19; women's role in, 55
Mossad, 76
Mothers, 74; adolescents' appraisal of, 100; choice of occupation and, 100; daughters feelings toward pregnancies of, 81–82; education and, 19, 49; idealization of, 67; influence of, 89, 99; maternal deprivation and, 68; *metaplot* relations with, 71–72, 105; nursing and, 68; psychological benefits of *metaplot* and, 107–108; quality of relationship with, 90; sex-role typing and, 29, *See also* Parent-child relationships
Moustakas, C.E., 108
Music, 96
Mussen, Paul, 28

Nagler, S., 52, 74, 101, 115–116
Nahalal, 4
Nathan, Michael, 78
Nazi concentration camps, 12
Neurotic parents, 75
Nursery schools, 23
Nursing mothers, 68, 71–72

Occupational choice, 100
Oedipal situation, 52, 92
Oranim, 24, 107
Oriental Jews, 115, 126

Orienting behavior, 111
Ownership, collective, 14–15

Palme, Olaf, 39, 40
Parent-child relationships, 67–104; adolescence and, 75–79; appraisal of relations in, 99; causes of friction in, 85–86, 100–102; children's attitudes toward time spent with, 84; differences between parents' and children's views in, 99–102; in early kibbutzim, 68–71; early research on, 79–82; economic dependence of children in, 70–71; evaluation of peer group in, 100; influence of age, sex and familism in, 96–99; main features of, 73–75; *metaplot* and, 113–119; misconceptions of role of, 67–68; in modern kibbutzim, 71–79; modern research on, 82–87; psychological needs of, 69; quality of relations between, 90–96; sleeping arrangements of children and, 83–84, 97, 98, 101; social style of, 72–73, 73–74; spheres of influence in, 87–90
Paths in Utopia (Buber), 6
Peers, 67–104; adolescence and, 76; attitudes toward time spent with, 84; parents' evaluation of, 100; problems of love and friendship and, 99; socialization of child and , 22, 73; spheres of influence in, 87–90
Personality development, 22–23
Political opinions, 87–88, 96, 97, 100
Pregnancy, 71, 81–82
Preschool age group, 24
Production, 128
Professional training for women, 55
Projection, 69, 116
Psychoanalytic school, 52, 69

Psychological factors: divorce and, 59, 60; education and, 21; *metaplot* and, 107–108; parents and, 69; youth movement and, 76
Psychosis, childhood, 24

Rabin, A.I., 68, 79, 116
Ramot, Lotte, 83, 108
Rapaport, E., 21
Repression, 78
Restitution money, 54
Role. *See* Sex-role typing
Ron-Polani, Y., 20, 32
Rosner, Menachem, 36
Rossi, Alice, 29, 36
Ruppin, Arthur, 17
Russia. *See* Soviet Russia
Russian Revolution of 1917, 8

Samuel, Edwin, 76
Sas, Ranaan, 119
Schmetterling, David, 45–46
Schnabel, Aliza, 78, 108
Science, 96
Second Aliyah, 4
Segal, M., 24
Self-defense, 33
Seminar HaKibbutzim, 24
Seventh Day, The (Near), 124, 125
Sex differences: adolescent acceptance of, 81; parent-child and peer group relationships and, 96–99, 101; role of women and, 31
Sex discrimination, 32–33
Sex-role typing: familistic tendencies and, 51–52; men's role in child-rearing and, 39–40; marriage and, 29–30; motherhood and, 29; women and, 27–30
Sexual division of work roles, 32–33, 34–37
Shapira, A., 73, 125
Shepher, Joseph, 31, 34, 37–38, 51–52
Shtetles, 46
Single persons, 60–61

Sleeping arrangements for children, 50–54, 83–84, 97, 98, 101
Smilanski, Moshe and Sarah, 74
Socialism: Kibbutz Artzi and, 10; kibbutz federations and, 8; kibbutzim organization and, 2, 17
Socialization: parent-child relationships and, 95; peer group in, 22, 73; sex-role typing and, 28–29, 42; in Soviet Russia, 69;
Social structure; appreciation of work and, 13–14; education and, 21–23; kibbutz and, 3, 16; kibbutz family and, 49–50; remarriage and, 60–61
Soviet Russia, 123; adolescent peer group studies in, 77; Buber and, 131, 132; changes in attitudes and, 38; early childhood education in, 105–106; gain motive in, 55; Kibbutz Artzi and, 11; kibbutz federations and, 8; socialization in, 69
Spiro, M., 16, 46
Spitz, R., 67
Ssedemot, 125–126
Stalin, Joseph, 123
Standard of living, 2
Sweden, 39–40

Tabenkin, Yizchak, 9, 20, 33
Talmon, Yonina, 15, 51, 53, 54, 56
Task orientation, 56–57
Taxation, 40
Teacher training, 24
Third Aliyah, 8, 21
Thomos, M.M., 45
Tiger, L., 31, 34, 37–38
Transference, 69
Trial marriage, 40
Trumpeldor, Y., 8, 9

Union of Collective Settlements, 7–8
United Kibbutz Movement, 8
U.S. immigrants, 64, 115

Voluntary service, 12

War, 124–125
Weber, Max, 15, 38
Werkleute, 131
"Why the Upbuilding of Palestine Has to Be Socialistic" (Buber), 133
Women, 27–44: attitudes toward early kibbutzim of, 20; attitude toward work of, 35–36; changing status quo for, 37–42; committee membership by, 51; in cooperative moshavim, 55; familistic tendencies and, 37–38, 53–54; household tasks and, 50; managerial positions of, 51; role in marriage of, 45; sex-role typing and, 27–30
Women's movement, 30
Work: diversification of women's, 41–42; parent-child relationship and, 92, 96; sexual division of roles in, 32–33, 34–37; social attitudes and appreciation of, 13–14
Wyneken, G., 21

Yaari, Meir, 10
Youth movement, 70, 76

Zionism, 8, 10

About the Author

Menachem Gerson, a disciple of Martin Buber, has played an important role in the Jewish Youth Movement. Born in Germany, Dr. Gerson emigrated to Israel in 1934, where he became a founding member of Kibbutz Hazorea. From 1940 to 1946 he was director of the Educational Department of Kibbutz Artzi, one of the three Kibbutz federations. From 1949 to 1951 he was an emissary of the Jewish Agency in London, where he worked with Zionist youth. From 1952 to 1973 Dr. Gerson was a member of the Board of Directors of Oranim, the School of Education of the kibbutz movement. He founded and was director of the Institute of Research on Kibbutz Education. In 1971 he served as a consultant to the Department of Psychiatry at the Albert Einstein College of Medicine at Bronx State Hospital. During that time he also gave guest lectures on kibbutz problems at Harvard University, Cornell University, the University of Michigan, and the National Institute of Mental Health. Dr. Gerson is the author of three other books, *A Way of Jewish Youth* (1934, German); *Fascism, Origin and Essence* (1939, Hebrew); and *Essays on Kibbutz Education* (1968, Hebrew).